Discovering the 5 Love Languages

AT SCHOOL

GRADES 1–6

Discovering the 5 Love Languages

AT SCHOOL

GRADES 1–6

*Lessons That Promote Academic
Excellence and Connections for Life*

GARY CHAPMAN, PhD
& D. M. FREED, MEd

NORTHFIELD PUBLISHING

CHICAGO

Contents

What Does Research Say?

CONNECTIONS MAKE ALL THE DIFFERENCE!

I have worked in school systems for over twenty years. I'm not new to education, and one thing I'm seeing these days is a widening gap between teachers and students. Teachers are working so hard to bring "best academic practices" to their students that it seems like they can hardly come up for air to get to "know" their students. I'm a true believer in best practices, and I believe that there should be research to support what we teach—this includes the creation of any lessons or curriculum, including ours. Without further ado, let me guide you through some important ideas about connections that I've discovered during my research about research.

I have sifted through tons of research that over and over again suggests that if students don't have strong connections with their teacher, they won't do well in the classroom, in the hallways, on the playground, riding the bus, eating lunch, making friends, and just about anything else you can think of that may help students achieve academically. And, while the connection with the teacher is important, let's not forget the research about connections regarding students and peers, students and family, and family with schools. I'd say, based on my research, connectedness between students and others is paramount to their success (first lesson learned)! When I mention my research to colleagues and that it says we need to be connecting with our students, they look at me dumbfounded and say, "Duh." If you are reading this and saying, "Duh," I completely understand. I know we really don't need research to understand this basic principle, but for the sake of being scholarly, let's head down "Research Road" together. My journey has left me encouraged and, more importantly, enlightened about what we need to be doing as educators. So let's get started by learning about the two types of positive connections that teachers need to make in the classroom.

There are two basic types of positive connections that teachers can make with students in the classroom. The first one we will call the "human connection." This is the connection that says from one human being to another, "I care about you. I'm glad you are in my classroom. I understand how you feel. I believe in you. We are on the same team. I think students are great! I respect you as a human being. Welcome to the planet! I will call you by your name when I talk with you."

The second one we will call the "academic connection." This one says, "We are here to learn about important and meaningful things. My teaching will bring you the best academic focus possible. My expectations for you are high. I know you can and will make great gains! Together we will challenge ideas and draw deeper meaning out of our discussions. I will make information clear, concise, and relevant. You can ask me questions. I won't waste your time."

So, on the one hand, we have the human connection and on the other, we have the academic connection. It's the combination of these two powerful connections that bring about the greatest academic achievement for students in the classroom. If we only connect with our students on the human level, we have no guarantee that their academic achievements will arrive. And, if we only connect with our students on an academic level, we will watch our students make smaller academic gains than they are capable of, which are highly likely to fall far below their full potential. Academic excellence and achievement happen at the crossroads of "human" and "academic" connection, a.k.a. your classroom.

Taking research into consideration, the five love language lessons are an example of human and academic connection in motion. When the lessons are completed, they establish the bridge of human connection between the student, teacher, and family. This connection carries over to all academic areas in the classroom. Teaching the 5 Love Languages creates understanding for students, educators, and families about what motivates them intrinsically. At the heart of what motivates us is what makes us feel loved. And understanding what makes ourselves and others feel loved meets the deepest of human needs for connection. When people feel connected at these levels, the learning environment transcends gender, race, religion, culture, behavior, economics, traumatic experiences, and ideological differences. The school environment becomes a safe and satisfying place to learn and ultimately opens the door to greater student effort. Effort is what students need to achieve their full academic potential.

The academic connection that is desired in a classroom comes through strong academic teaching and lessons, lessons that draw focus to what's important and dig out deeper meanings. This includes questions, problems, interactions, and discussions that cause the student to think deeper and require the teacher to interact with the student on that level. The Academic Focus Pages (AFPs) that accompany these lessons have been created to bring focus to what is being taught in ways that are appropriate, relevant, and effective at each grade level, as well as to cause deeper thinking. The majority of the questions and approaches are based on research found in the book *Classroom Instruction that Works* (Dean, Hubbell, Pitler, and Stone, 2012). Their book describes research-based strategies for increasing student achievement and, yes, cites studies done that support the importance of student-teacher relationships including higher-order thinking. This is why you will find the AFPs with learning objectives, advance organizers, compare/contrast, non-examples, linguistic and nonlinguistic representations, questions to draw prior knowledge, and much more. Even the five love language lessons themselves are taught in a compare/contrast format so that students can readily identify "what to do" as opposed to "what not to do."

When we talk about teachers connecting in two different ways with their students, it should be understood that academic connection (best practice) doesn't stop or end with the love language lessons alone. The love language lessons have been intentionally developed to combine and create the two powerful connections in your classroom while you teach them. However, our primary goal is to provide lessons that create the "human connection" between student and educator while they interact together during the use of high-quality academic instruction in all other areas. Think of the love language lessons as one half of the equation to bring about the complete connection in the classroom throughout the school year.

Okay, that's as simple as I can explain the research and application, but you don't have to rely on my word alone. Examples of great research that's already been done over the years is available to support what I've just said and a whole lot more. There are literally thousands of studies that support connections in all of its various forms. Limiting the research to just a few was challenging. Much of the information I've cited can be easily accessed online in its entirety. Once you start reading the research from these few examples, I think you will be amazed at the studies and asking yourself, as I did, "Why aren't we focusing more on human connections across the board?" It's truly one of the most inexpensive ways to increase academic achievement and significantly impact others positively for life.

As you read the various research that I've cited, you will see that it says, "Key Findings . . ." I've tried to directly quote or write a simple summary from the paper, study, research, or book that will enable you to quickly know what to expect if you want to dig deeper. The references I've cited are mostly juried, so you won't be wasting your time with information that is "opinion" or trendy. It's research that's been given the nod by other experts or professionals in the area being discussed. I've narrowed it down to a few examples that I think clearly support the concept of the *Discovering the 5 Love Languages* curriculum.

There's so much more to be learned than I've presented as examples of exemplary research. I hope you will take the time to look into some of these studies, visit the websites, or use their resources. They cover many other areas of research, which will increase any educator's effectiveness in the classroom. The information will build a firm foundation for your understanding as it relates to teaching the five love language lessons. Enjoy!

—D. M. Freed

Educational Connectedness Research

THE IMPORTANCE OF STUDENT-TEACHER CONNECTIONS

Visible Learning: A Synthesis of Over 800 Meta-Analyses Relating to Achievement by John Hattie

KEY FINDINGS: The relationship between teacher and student plays a vital role for increasing academic achievement. John Hattie ranks it as 11/138 based on the effect size (d=.72), which indicates that this should make teacher-student relationships one of the highest priorities. This book is considered by some to be the "gold standard" for many areas of educational impact. It is based on the compilation of over 50,000 studies and millions of students.

Hattie, John. *Visible Learning: A Synthesis of Over 800 Meta-Analyses Relating to Achievement.* New York: Routledge, 2009.

Classroom Instruction that Works: Research-Based Strategies for Increasing Student Achievement by Ceri B. Dean, Elizabeth Ross Hubbell, Howard Pitler, and BJ Stone

KEY FINDINGS: Academic connections in the classroom come from research-based strategies that contribute to positive student-teacher relationships. The folks at McRel knock it out of the park with their book that looks at teaching strategies that have the most positive effect on student learning. Their many strategies, which include opportunities for higher-order thinking, create academic connections between teacher and student. They also cite the research of John Hattie from Visible Learning. This is a must-have book for any educator.

Dean, Ceri, et al. *Classroom Instruction that Works: Research-Based Strategies for Increasing Student Achievement.* 2nd ed. Denver: Association for Supervision & Curriculum Development, 2012.

"Relationships Matter: Linking Teacher Support to Student Engagement and Achievement" by Adena M. Klem and James P. Connell

KEY FINDINGS: "These results indicate teacher support is important to student engagement in school as reported by students and teachers. Students who perceive teachers as creating a caring, well-structured learning environment in which expectations are high, clear and fair are more likely to report engagement in school. In turn, high levels of engagement are associated with higher attendance and test scores." (Klem and Connell, 270)

Klem, Adena M., and James P. Connell. "Relationships Matter: Linking Teacher Support to Student Engagement and Achievement." *Journal of School Health* 74, no. 7 (2004): 262–273.

"Liking or Disliking the Teacher: Student Motivation, Engagement and Achievement" by Gregory P. Montalvo, Eric A. Mansfield, and Raymond B. Miller

KEY FINDINGS: A study done with students who liked and disliked their teachers. Research produced findings that students who like their teachers are more likely to experience motivational and achievement benefits.

Montalvo, Gregory P., Eric A. Mansfield, and Raymond B. Miller. "Liking or Disliking the Teacher: Student Motivation, Engagement and Achievement." *Evaluation and Research in Education* 20, no. 3 (2007): 144–158.

THE IMPORTANCE OF STUDENT-STUDENT CONNECTIONS

"Classroom Social Experiences as Predictors of Academic Performance" by Lisa Flook, Rena L. Repetti, and Jodie B. Ullman

KEY FINDINGS: "The results of this study suggest that problems with peer acceptance in the classroom are of legitimate concern to schools. Peer problems affect children's self-concept, mental health, and consequently, performance in school. First, the results replicate findings from previous studies linking problematic peer relations with academic performance. Children who were perceived by their teachers as lacking acceptance by their peers demonstrated poorer academic outcomes. A lack of peer acceptance explained as much as one fourth of the variance in academic performance." (Flook, Repetti, and Ullman, 324–325)

Flook, Lisa, Rena L. Repetti, and Jodie B. Ullman. "Classroom Social Experiences as Predictors of Academic Performance." *Developmental Psychology* 41, no. 2 (2005): 319–327.

Handbook of Peer Interactions, Relationships, and Groups edited by Kenneth H. Rubin, William M. Bukowski, and Brett Laursen

KEY FINDINGS: This book identifies various types of research reviewed by experts regarding peer interactions and much more (as the title suggests). Chapter 29, "Peers and Academic Functioning at School," written and reviewed by Kathryn R. Wentzel, cites the direct correlation between peers and academic achievement. A variety of research is cited that demonstrates that when students perceive they are being supported and cared for by other students they have "positive academic outcomes." (Wentzel, 537)

Wentzel, Kathryn R. "Peers and Academic Functioning at School" in *Handbook of Peer Interactions, Relationships, and Groups*, edited by Rubin, Kenneth H., William M. Bukowski, and Brett Laursen, 531–547. New York: The Guilford Press, 2011.

"The Impact of Children's Social Adjustment on Academic Outcomes" by Melissa E. DeRosier and Stacey W. Lloyd

KEY FINDINGS: This amazing study uses measurements to determine academic outcomes based on social adjustment. For this study, it separates social adjustment into two categories: social acceptance and aggression. The study further looks at classroom conduct, academic performance, academic help-seeking, academic self-concept, and absenteeism as it relates to the focus of the study. The authors, Melissa E. DeRosier and Stacey W. Lloyd, have made it very easy to understand and include data to support their research.

DeRosier, Melissa E., and Stacey W. Lloyd. "The Impact of Children's Social Adjustment on Academic Outcomes." *Reading and Writing Quarterly* 27, no. 1–2 (2010): 25–47.

THE IMPORTANCE OF STUDENT-PARENT-SCHOOL CONNECTIONS

"Readiness: School, Family, and Community Connections" (Annual Synthesis 2004) by Martha Boethel

KEY FINDINGS: Description of forty-eight research studies that describe school, family, and community connections as they relate to school readiness. Of particular interest, there are descriptions within these research studies that discuss the need for quality family relationships and interactions, which include emotional well-being, love, and nurturing. These studies are focused on early childhood, but I feel that they have relevance to all grade levels as students don't lose their need for quality family interactions as they get older. I've always appreciated the information provided by SEDL over the years. They write information in a format that is clear, concise, researched, and practical for all educators. Much of their material can be accessed online (www.sedl.org) if you are willing to be on their email list. Well worth it!

Boethel, Martha. "Readiness: School, Family, & Community Connections." Austin: Southwest Educational Development Laboratory (SEDL), 2004.

Comer School Development Program

KEY FINDINGS: Dr. James Comer, M.D., from Yale, started the School Development Program (SDP) in 1968. He started with one school and has since turned it into a national model. Their vision is for the total development of all children by creating learning environments that support children's physical, cognitive, psychological, language, social, and ethical development. Their model has been shown to significantly close achievement gaps. One of their core beliefs is, "Children's most meaningful learning occurs through positive and supportive relationships with caring and nurturing adults." Their work addresses the need for children to build relationships with parents, educators, and other adults amid many other practical applications. Is it any wonder Dr. Comer is a hero of mine? Their website contains a wealth of information and research links for educators.

Comer School Development Program
http://medicine.yale.edu/childstudy/comer/index.aspx

Center on School, Family, and Community Partnerships

KEY FINDINGS: Joyce Epstein, the director of John Hopkins University, is a leading expert on the topic of connecting schools with family and community. "The mission of this Center is to conduct and disseminate research, programs, and policy analyses that produce new and useful knowledge and practices that help parents, educators, and members of communities work together to improve schools, strengthen families, and enhance student learning and development." Their focus on connecting and strengthening families coincides with our vision as one of the many benefits the five love language curriculum offers. Their website has incredible information for all educators and families.

Center on School, Family, and Community Partnerships
www.csos.jhu.edu/p2000/center.htm

Welcome to the Love Languages

Welcome to what I hope are some of the greatest lessons you will ever teach.

When I first taught the five love languages in our school, I wasn't sure how it would go over. But if you receive the same praise and positive responses from parents, students, and staff that I did, you will agree that it's a highly satisfactory experience!

Let me tell you about this exciting curriculum and how I came to use it. At the time, my elementary school had the third largest population in our district, with only two high schools that were larger. I had approximately 700 students to attend to as their only school counselor. Time was one thing I didn't have. As you can imagine in a school of this size, there are a variety of needs that, quite honestly, go unaddressed. Finding myself mainly triaging "problem students," I kept feeling like I was missing out on the rest of the students, the ones who don't have a lot of problems but still need to be invested in. Overall, I wanted to find a curriculum that would help students get along better, help teachers understand and connect with students, meet our district requirements in areas such as bullying, harassment, unsafe touch, and diversity, and on top of everything else, help improve academic skills! Sound like an impossible goal? I thought so too.

As I searched through different types of curriculum, I found that most of the materials were either too advanced or too simplistic for my students. Or the materials addressed some of the areas but not others. When I teach a lesson, I want it to be meaningful and have some meat to it. I look for lessons that are realistic, practical, easy to understand, and have an impact on everyone from the students' families to the district office. That's when it hit me! Love. That's right, I said it. Love.

I have been in education for a number of years, and, as you may know, we don't use the L-word very often at school. We tell students to care, show respect, be considerate, be kind, help others, and a variety of other things, but we rarely, if ever, use the L-word. All of these things are great for students to do, but really, don't they all stem from one thing, love? I have not gone off the deep end or attempted to reenter the hippie era. Stay with me.

I think the reason we don't use the word "love" in education is because the word comes with all sorts of romantic notions. We fall in love, we are in love, we are "lovey-dovey," and a host of other things. It almost seems that if love isn't connected to romance, it becomes null and void. Should we be surprised that when the word is used, small children scrunch their faces uncomfortably and men run? Love has been so commercialized that we have literally allowed marketers to tell us, for their financial gain, what love is. So much of what we know about love is defined by marketers that many of us have forgotten what love actually is!

Sadly, if adults lose sight of what love is, so will the children. The children of this generation are even more prone to making decisions based on media than many of us were when we were kids. Never has there been a greater push to target our young people for commercial purposes. Venues such as the Internet, literature, movie theaters, television, and even sports stadiums are phenomenal commercial outlets. Is it any wonder we don't use the word "love" at school? Based on the marketers' definition, you would have to be insane to sell that word to school-age children!

But the good news is we aren't marketers. We are educators who are driven, or at least should be driven, to bring the truth to our students for their benefit, especially when the truth will surely affect every aspect of their lives. I don't care what race, religion, country, or planet you are from, love will affect your life one way or another. With the profound information that is found in the love languages, we have an opportunity to help generations of students understand one another better than ever before. This understanding will permeate many facets of their lives and create connections that most of us have never even dreamed of. Are you starting to get the picture? I did. That is how this curriculum came about. I hope you are excited about this adventure, but first, let's get started on a working definition of love that will make sense for us to use.

Is love a noun, a verb, or both? It is an interesting word because it can take on many different forms. With a few tweaks here and there, you might even be able to pull an adjective out of it. Who knows? But one thing is for certain, your students have heard it used in just about every possible way. Love is passed around in some homes on a daily basis like salt on a dinner table. It's our job to "rein it in," "bring the spotlight to it," "get it under control," and "give it some teeth." We have to enable love to be what it was meant to be . . . powerful! No more washed-out, casual love. We are going to give it the definition it deserves. And we shall call it . . . a verb.

Okay, that was a lot of lead-in just to conclude, "Let's call it a verb," but I really want you to understand what is going through students' heads and just about everyone else's heads when they think about this innocuous little word. In order for us to be effective in our teaching of these lessons, we all have to agree that the word "love" shall be used as a verb.

With love as a verb, it definitely has to become an action word, which means that those who are using it will be doing something. That "something" is really important. Students will think that it's odd at first to hear you use the L-word, and will of course have their own definition. You must prevail and overcome their preconceived notions with a comprehensive lesson (see Lesson 1) that helps put things into perspective. You may even find yourself having to set aside your own prejudice and rethink this word. As I said earlier, it's not very common for educators to wield this word, and for good reasons. Most are uncomfortable because they don't really know how it would be used in the classroom, let alone in any kind of meaningful lesson format. Seriously, when was the last time you heard yourself or a fellow educator say to a child, "And how are you loving him?"

Three of the greatest advantages that these lessons have over others are: (1) they are new and refreshing in an area that is research based, (2) they build incredible connections, and (3) they are powerful. Notice that I use that word "powerful" again. Powerful because even though everybody has their own definition of love, just about everyone can relate to it. I say just about everyone because I know there are the very rare exceptions in the world where people are biologically unable to relate. For our purposes, however, we will assume everyone in your school/class has the capacity to show and receive love. It's really exciting when you teach a child something that is so intrinsic that it makes a genuine impact at all age levels with the deepest of heartfelt understanding. I know. I've done it! And so will you.

The first day I taught the love languages curriculum, I knew that we were on to something good, but little did I realize how good it would be until the next day. A parent caught me at the front door of our school in the morning and said, "Mr. Freed, thank you for teaching my child about love. She was so excited and can't wait to learn the other love languages." These types of compliments came pouring in through phone calls, conversations, and emails. And it didn't stop there. As the languages became more involved and the students really started understanding what love is, I received compliments every day for seven weeks! Now, I don't know about you, but I truly can't remember the last time I taught anything that had more than three people saying something nice. As I said, you know when you are on to something good.

That's what teaching these languages does. It takes students, staff, and parents to a whole new level of understanding about themselves and others. We saw the dynamics of teacher/student relationships change. We saw child/parent relationships change. In every case, the changes were for the better. And not just change, in every case for the better—not change for its own sake, but with deep meaning. Something amazing happens when you know you are teaching a curriculum that will affect a student for life, in every aspect of his or her life. I will tell you some remarkable stories later as we address each language individually, and I guarantee you will be impressed. I know I sound fanatically excited, and I am. My excitement wells from the experiences I have had from teaching these lessons many times! My experiences have changed my life forever.

The first class I taught was a bunch of rambunctious fourth grade students. With all of them sitting at their desks ready to learn, I announced loudly, "Today we are going to talk about love!" From the look on the students' faces, I'd say we had just entered a lemon-eating contest and everyone was attempting to win at the same time. There were "ughs" and "nooooooooos" proclaimed throughout the class. I stood quietly until the last lemon was eaten and said, "Are you ready to learn about love?" The class was silent this time as the truth sank in: "We really are going to learn about love."

Elementary students are typically thought of as "takers" because they have a high need to be taken care of in ways that they just can't do for themselves. It's okay for children to be "takers" when the context is right. That's the way things work in the world. Children take and adults give, and give, and give, and give some more until they have raised the child into adulthood. Unfortunately, I think we fall into this "children are takers" attitude a bit too much sometimes. When we forget that children, or anyone for that matter, can be better than they are, we limit their potential. It's not surprising that in the area of love, children are often allowed to be exempt. The love we expect from them is usually no more than a random act of kindness. It might take the form of a kind word, sitting on the couch with us, breakfast in bed, a gift, or a hug. These expressions of love are often prompted by other people, but not always. In fact, at times these expressions of love happen completely on their own. How can this be? Have they observed these behaviors and they are emulating them? Maybe, but I think that they come by them intrinsically.

There are basically five different ways people can show or receive love. These "Love Languages" were identified and brought to light by Gary Chapman in his first book, written for married couples. Gary, a counselor, discovered that many couples simply didn't feel loved by one another. A recurrent theme between the couples he was counseling was that while they wanted to show their love for each other, husbands and wives seemed to be speaking "different languages" and were failing miserably at understanding each other. They either didn't know how to love their mate, or they were trying to love their mate in a way that didn't make them feel loved. His keen observations led him to see that people show love and receive love in five key areas. It is from these observations that we derive the basis for our curriculum. And, not surprisingly, we find that all people, not just married couples, show or receive love in these five areas.

You may be wondering as I did at one point in time, "Are there really only five ways to show love and receive it?" The answer, oddly, is yes. Everything we do to show people that we love them falls into one of these five key areas or love languages. They are: (1) words of affirmation, (2) quality time, (3) acts of service, (4) gifts, and (5) touch. When I first heard about these, I racked my brain, as many others have, trying to find the exception. It can't be done. Go ahead, try . . . I know you want to. . . . Okay, finished? Now let's take a closer look at this curriculum.

Since there are only five love languages, it begins to make perfect sense that we must start teaching these to students. Just as math is straightforward and constant, so are the five love languages. It's strange to think that a subject like love can be quantified, but in this case, it truly can! Because we can empirically say there are only five love languages, we are able to form a firm foundation for our curriculum. As you know, curriculum needs to be straightforward, easy to understand, applicable, assessable, and, most importantly, true. Just like in the teaching of math, reading, or writing, we must have ways to gauge whether or not our students are comprehending and mastering the material. A good curriculum should always have a way to do assessment. The problem with most "life skill" type lessons is that they have a good message but aren't very assessable. This doesn't mean that they aren't worth teaching or true or good or helpful, but it does make it hard to justify why we are teaching them. And, I might add, we do still teach these lessons from time to time because we know in our hearts it's the right thing to do.

Teaching the love languages doesn't require you to step out on a shaking limb. The very nature of it demonstrates all of the aspects of any other solid curriculum. It's a curriculum that will work at virtually any age level and ability, provided that the student can learn. The Academic Focus Pages were created to bring focus to the lessons in ways that are researched-based. The questions, cues, advanced organizers, linguistic and non-linguistic representations, compare/contrast, example/non-example, and note pages are all based on strong research (Dean, Hubbell, Pitler & Stone, 2010), to bring you the best results possible and to cause deeper thinking.

You can expect to see a variety of things happen as you proceed through these lessons. Students will begin to develop a sense of self and an awareness of those around them. It will seem strange as you hear stories about how, for the first time, they practiced loving people and the responses they received. They will start changing the way they relate to each other, and there will be plenty of opportunity to reinforce this on a daily basis.

You will find that you relate to your students differently. That's right, I said you. This curriculum changes the instructor. As you get more into these lessons and discover the students' love languages, you will begin to understand what motivates them. You will begin to understand what motivates you! Staff members start relating differently to each other as they start talking about their love languages. It's the natural thing to do. Your overall experience will be wonderful and transforming as you all learn to speak the different languages. There are many more ways you can use this curriculum, and I will be covering those in later chapters. It's a curriculum that meets many, many needs of everyone in the building—from students with learning and behavioral difficulties to students identified as "exceptional." The halo effect is amazing! So let's take a look at some general guidelines and suggestions on how to use and teach these lessons effectively.

CHAPTER 1

How to Use
This Curriculum

GENERAL GUIDELINES

When you begin teaching these lessons, you can expect a variety of responses. Remember that most administrators, students, teachers, and parents have never heard the word "love" used in an academic setting. It is very likely that they have never been taught a working definition of "love," although many of them will have heard of Gary Chapman's book *The 5 Love Languages: The Secret to Love That Lasts*. And why wouldn't they? As of 2014, he had sold over 9 million copies! With this in mind, it is very important that you set the stage so that everyone can be on board with what you are about to teach.

Some school districts require curriculum review/adoption before you are allowed to teach different types of materials. A suggestion before you start is to get permission from your principal or district office. The beauty of this material is that it is so versatile, you can use it without it being a curriculum. When I use the word "curriculum," in this instance, I'm talking about making it mandatory material to be taught in every classroom or specific grade level at your school. Most districts agree that mandatory curriculum is something that teachers must teach because it has been adopted by the school board and is going to be taught to all or certain groups of students for a prescribed period of time. Therefore, mandatory curriculum is usually taught to a captive audience. It wouldn't surprise me if you easily gained approval from your district to make this mandatory curriculum. Current research clearly indicates that a student's highest level of academic success hinges on a significant connection with an adult in the school (preferably the teacher).

School district personnel have always known this fact but until now, have had very few options for a curriculum that "fits the bill."

For clarification, as you are reading the different sections of this book, if I use the word "curriculum," it can either mean curriculum that your district chooses to adopt permanently or curriculum you choose to use as support material for whatever your district currently requires. I say this to answer any questions regarding whether this is curriculum or support material; the answer is either/or. But I will be referring to it as the "love language curriculum" for simplicity.

Should I Team-Teach?

Team-teaching these lessons is not required to achieve excellent results, but working with a specialist can produce excellent results with the added benefit of allowing your students the opportunity to make yet another significant connection in the classroom. The lessons are designed to connect students with the teacher, each other, and their families. I think the perfect arrangement would be for the teacher and specialist to work together. Teachers gain the benefit of connecting with their students on the love language level, and specialists connect with students on the personal safety level. Regardless of whether you are the teacher or specialist bringing these lessons to the classroom, try to include each other if possible. The act of working together is a great example for students to witness positive connections in action and for them to make another significant connection with an adult in the school.

These suggestions have been written with the understanding that this curriculum is going out to a lot of different school settings with a variety of personnel situations. Unfortunately, not everyone is afforded the luxury of a specialist/school counselor. Remember the heading says "General Guidelines." The design of these lessons gives you many options, and you should use the one(s) that work best at your school. For example, if your district has its own adopted curriculum for reporting bullying, harassment, etc., then any one of the personal safety lessons can be replaced with the district's approved curriculum that coincides.

Let Everyone Know the Lesson Objectives

Let parents know your objectives for teaching these lessons. To inform parents, I've written a letter (See Appendix 1) you can copy and use. Most people don't have a working definition of love. After you give them one, everybody will be able to breathe a little easier and realize you are about to embark on something great that will increase the potential for students to reach their full academic achievement.

If you are a specialist and don't have to have the teacher's permission before you teach in their classroom or aren't planning on team teaching, they should still be apprised of the lesson objectives. Having the support of the teacher is very important since these lessons will impact their classroom significantly, and they should be provided the opportunity to be included. Once teachers see how this material changes the lives of students and staff, they will understand the huge benefit of knowing their students' love languages, but until then, keep them informed.

You Have a Love Language!

"Know Thyself" was the motto carved in stone on the entrance of the school founded by Greek philosopher Plato. I think Plato was on to something. One thing I'm really convinced of is this: whoever teaches these lessons really needs to have a handle on this material as it applies to him or herself. You are about to teach something that is applicable to every human alive. This includes you. Sometimes instructors don't like to talk about themselves, or anything personal for that matter. Sometimes this is good. But for the most part, people who simply teach material are mostly boring and don't connect with students on a human level. More importantly, it makes it hard for students, especially children, to relate to the person who is teaching it. Love language material is very personal. It is about how you show and receive love. It's about making connections with your students. So be thinking about how you show and receive love.

You have a love language of your own, maybe even two. Discovering your love language is necessary before you teach this material. It would be great if you can present, as appropriate, times and situations where you became aware of your love languages. When I teach, I use stories about myself that are current or about when I was a kid. I will elaborate more on how I teach when we get to the actual lessons. Students want to see you model your pride in and awareness of your own love languages. Your example encourages them to identify their own. It makes it okay to have a love language. Read through this material, get a grip on your love languages, jot down some notes about your life that are funny or interesting, and make it personal. Well, not too personal. I don't think any students want to hear about how you discovered that quality time wasn't your love language after you got a divorce. Use common sense. Laugh a lot.

Be ready for staff and parents in a good way. I can't tell you how many times staff members told me that they really looked forward to my coming in and teaching every year. Many adults use this information for what it was originally intended for—their marriages. Parents are in the same category. Students will go home and teach the lessons to their parents, and you will discover parents craving to know the information for their own marriage or life. As a result, you will receive many requests for books and information regarding this material. You may want to have copies of Gary's original book written for couples and perhaps Gary and Dr. Ross Campbell's book that helps parents discover their child's love language.

For Specialists

Previously I said, "Know Thyself." But also, "Know Thy Staff." If you are a specialist and teach from room to room, be sure that you know your teachers and prepare them to be included. I often have teachers help me out in the classroom to act out scenes that demonstrate ways to show or receive love. This is not a curriculum where teachers should be absent during your presentation (see chapter on research). This material includes EVERYBODY. Teachers will be making reference to this material as they deal with students on a daily basis. It won't be a difficult thing to do. They will simply refer to it naturally. If they aren't in the room while you are teaching or using the lesson time as a prep period, they will miss out on a great deal. Plus, parents will have loads of questions for them, and they will want to be in the know. Also, because every love language has an opposite that has relevance for school and district policies, teachers will want to be present for these as well. It documents for them that key issues were addressed in their classroom before an incident occurs. There will be times when students misbehave or break school rules. Being able to check their attendance record and confirm that they were present for the lessons helps to shape the conversation toward what they learned to do rather than what they did wrong. Using the lessons as a talking point will go a long way toward correcting inappropriate behaviors.

Thanks for Following the Rules!

Presenting the lessons that are opposite of the love languages will certainly make your administrators and school district happy. Let me explain why. Earlier I said that this material can be used as curriculum (permanent) or a venue for support material. Here's how that works in general. All five of the love languages are positive ways to show and receive love. The bulk of the time spent during the lessons is focused on the positives or "what you should do," as opposed to "what you shouldn't do." However, with every love language lesson taught, the opposite to that lesson is also taught for compare/contrast. It's these opposite lessons that virtually all districts are required to address at some point during the school year. These areas are typically covered to keep the school safe and to fulfill the obligations of the district legally. The love language lessons are incredible for schools in this way. They cover the required areas while focusing on the positive things that students should be doing. In only a few short weeks with minimal amounts of time, all district areas are covered in depth at least once. The areas that most districts cover with some sort of curriculum are: harassment, exclusion, bullying/reporting, bringing illegal or inappropriate items to school, manipulation, and unsafe touch/child abuse. All of these topics fall under the category of "personal safety." The love language material specifically addresses personal safety issues during each of the lessons.

Remember when they taught you in college that compare/contrast was a higher level of thinking than true/false? By instructing with compare/contrast you will cover both the positive side of the love languages (what to do) and the opposite (what not to do). When a teacher presents with the compare/contrast method, students have both sides laid out before them. The picture is much clearer and students make better connections. We are all about the connections! Love languages focus on the positive and "what to do" rather than the negative. When students start applying the love languages to their lives, then they won't be conducting themselves in unsafe ways. Students will know what to do and how to conduct themselves in their relationships with others. This will go on for a lifetime, not just at school.

NUTS AND BOLTS

Teaching the five love languages at the beginning of the school year is a good idea because these lessons have been created to build connections (read the chapter on research regarding connections). I typically teach the love languages over seven weeks, on occasion have taught them over eight, and sometimes in as few as six. To be really thorough, seven is ideal. This is especially true for your first run at it. I'm sure there will be some who would like to teach these lessons but may be extremely limited in the amount of days available to them. My thinking is, it's better to teach the material than not. The lessons could be taught back-to-back over seven days, but the students may lose the benefit of doing the school-home assignments. These lessons have been written for educators who are located in school settings and hopefully have enough time to teach them according to design. For those of you in other settings, e.g., summer camps, you will find it easy to edit the lessons according to your needs.

This book and curriculum have been written in such a way that the lessons are short and to the point. I don't want educators to have to wade through pages of babble. Each chapter and lesson has been designed to be meaningful and efficient. The lessons are rarely longer than forty-five minutes and are often shorter. The exceptions are the seventh and eighth lessons. Both of these may require sixty minutes due to the intensity, activities, and nature of the information. In chapter 7, I have suggested that you may want to teach it in two parts. This, of course, would create the need for another day of teaching. You will have to decide which works best for you after reading the material.

Each chapter starts out with an introduction. The introduction contains information that is vital to the lesson plan. Within the introduction you will find background information, the significance of that particular love language, educational philosophy, and, in some cases, pitfalls to avoid. While reading the introduction, you may want to underline key points or ideas. The introduction will give you a base of understanding that clarifies how the lesson is supposed to flow.

There are two styles of lesson plans provided for each lesson. The first lesson plan is scripted and written in **bold** letters. For the most part, you could literally sit down with your students and read it to them word for word. Within the scripted lesson plan there are (*italicized words in parentheses*); these appear after a question and will provide you with an answer or give directions to an action that must be performed. On occasion, the word (*rhetorical*) in parentheses will follow a question; this simply means what it suggests: the question is being asked to provoke thought. Other words are within [brackets]. Words within brackets contain ideas or thoughts that will be useful to the instructor but don't necessarily require any action.

Having scripted lesson plans provides a wonderful advantage. It gives you the opportunity to read the actual words that I used while teaching the lessons many times. As I mentioned earlier, you can read these lesson plans to the students word for word and it will work, but this isn't my suggested approach. Rather, I would recommend that you read the scripted lesson plan over a few times, get a good feel for the lesson, and use the abbreviated lesson plan for teaching. Reading a scripted lesson plan can be done, but it tends to lose spontaneity and doesn't sound original. Having said all of this, I do believe that there are times when you really should read the scripted lesson plan and not use the other format.

Scripted lesson plans are excellent, direct instruction. They keep the students and the instructor focused on arriving at the objectives. Here are some times when a scripted lesson plan can be very beneficial:

1. When you need to use direct instruction that doesn't meander.
2. When there hasn't been enough time to prepare.
3. When you are uncomfortable with the information and fear that you might miss crucial points.
4. When you are completely new to teaching, not a teacher at all, or feel that you can teach the scripted lessons as if they were your own words.

The second lesson plan format is an abbreviated style. The abbreviated lesson plan follows the scripted lesson plan, highlighting key points and giving directions. Each point is sequentially numbered and correlates with a paragraph in the scripted lesson plan. For example, the numbers 1, 2, 3, and 4 may be grouped at the beginning of a lesson plan indicating that these points are found in the first paragraph of the scripted lesson plan. The scripted lesson plan can be used to give insight on key points where more clarification is needed.

Both types of lesson plans have been written with six main components:

1. Objective (which includes student targets)
2. Review
3. Anticipatory Set
4. Teaching/Presentation
5. Closure
6. Independent Practice

To recap, the best way to teach these lessons is:

1. Read each chapter introduction thoroughly, underlining key points and thoughts.
2. Preread the scripted lesson plan several times to get a feel for the flow, paying special attention to (answers) and (directions).
3. Read the "Final Thoughts" section, which will add depth to the lesson plan after you have read and understood it.
4. Read "From the Classroom" for inspiration.
5. Use the abbreviated lesson plan for teaching. Insert your own stories, school procedures, and ideas.

The Academic Focus Pages bring tremendous focus to the lessons and cement the concepts for students. The variety of cues, questions, etc., will bring deeper understanding and greater meaning. A lot of time and research went into the construction and implementation of the AFPs.

The remaining chapters provide equally important material. In chapter 9, you will find information about how to use the data that is generated from the lessons. Each person has unique needs for this material. For example, counselors will use it when a child comes in for help. A school nurse will use the information to help treat a child who frequently visits the health room. Teachers will use the information to motivate and connect with the class, and administrators will use it to assess the climate of their school, address behavior issues from a positive point of view, and be able to document that school safety was covered across the board in a thorough way.

And for those of you who are required to meet Common Core State Standards, we've provided documentation to present to your school district or principal (see appendix 2). The lessons themselves cover a variety of areas for ELA: Speaking and Listening in all six grade levels.

CHAPTER 2

Introducing the Love Languages

INTRODUCTION

As I've already related, I walked into a fourth grade classroom to deliver my first love language lesson ever. I was more excited than nervous to embark on this adventure. The first thing I told them was, "Today we are going to talk about LOVE." I thought the shock value would heighten their sense of awareness and tune them in to my very important message. One thing was for sure, it heightened their sense of awareness.

From the moans and groans in that classroom as I let those words fly from my mouth, I thought I had entered a cattle yard. There were ooooos and awwwws, sneers and huhs. I stood silent, and eventually you could hear nervous laughter. It was sinking in . . . he's serious! Some people may say I'm a prankster and, of course, that's why I introduced the lesson this way. (Others say ingenious, but I will leave that up to you.)

When the laughter and chatter subsided, someone asked the question, "Are we supposed to learn about love?" I knew when that question was asked that I had them. The class was silent and waiting for this very enlightened questioner to be answered. "Well, that depends on what you think the definition of love is. What do you think the definition of love is?" This fourth grader (a boy, I might add) stumbled around his words until somebody jumped in to help him and said what many were thinking, "Isn't that about kissing and stuff, like a boyfriend/girlfriend thing?" Now was my chance to reel them in. "How many of you think I would be in here to teach you about how to date? Give you some good advice on 'going out' with someone?" The whole class laughed at the absurdity. Then another student asked the golden question, "Then what is the definition of love?"

"Ah!" I said. "I'm glad you asked." I proceeded to tell them about how love was a verb, an action word. What they may have originally thought was love was actually "romance."

There is a very big difference indeed and, not surprisingly, these concepts are confused by most children and many adults.

Let me take a break at this point and remind you that it is this confusion between romance and love that has caused such a problem in society. For example, many people who by nature tend to shy away from romance will inevitably throw out love as well, viewing both as just a bunch of "mushy garbage." These thoughts that persist among each of us are regularly reinforced by various types of media and form the first obstacle to a proper understanding of how to show and receive love. Once we have helped anyone understand the difference between romance and the five love languages, the door will open wide, and the relevance will be obvious. Having said this, it becomes really important that we make these differences clear to our students so they can start putting love into practice.

IMPORTANT TO KNOW!

The following love language lesson can be taught by itself or you may choose to teach the Words of Affirmation lesson (chapter 3) immediately after. It wasn't included with the Words of Affirmation chapter to create a clear understanding regarding the objectives to be taught.

LESSON 1
The True Meaning of "Love"
(SCRIPTED)

OBJECTIVE:

Students will understand that the five love languages are unique and involve action. Specifically, students will have a working definition of the word "love" as it is used in these lessons (i.e., it is a "verb" or "action word"). Further, students will understand that there is a difference between love and romance.

On the white board, set objectives:

1. I can define the word "love" as it is used in these lessons.
2. I can describe the difference between love and romance.

(Have students talk with each other for thirty seconds about what they think they are going to be learning today.)

ANTICIPATORY SET:

Instructor: "Today I am going to teach you about love." *(wait for student reactions) Say to them,* **"What is your definition of love?"**

Grade 1 or 2, continue here:	Lesson 1.0, Grade 1–2, #1

Have students draw their picture and write sentences. Remember these lessons have been designed for you to have students write more or less depending on their ability and grade level. Have students share with a partner, and then ask for volunteers to share with the class.

LESSON 1
The True Meaning of "Love"
(ABBREVIATED)

OBJECTIVE:

Students will understand that the five love languages are unique and involve action. Specifically, students will have a working definition of the word "love" as it is used in these lessons (i.e., it is a "verb" or "action word"). Further, students will understand that there is a difference between love and romance.

On the white board, set objectives:

1. I can define the word "love" as it is used in these lessons.
2. I can describe the difference between love and romance.

(Have students talk with each other for thirty seconds about what they think they are going to be learning today.)

ANTICIPATORY SET:

1. "Today I'm going to teach you about love."

2. Ask students about their definition.
   • **Academic Focus Page [Lesson 1.0, Grades 1–2 and 5–6, #1]**

3. Make it clear you are not there to teach about how to date, and so on.

4. Inform them that you will be teaching them something that they can use for the rest of their lives.

AFP: Lesson 1.0, Grade 1–2, #1

Name _____ Date _____   **LESSON 1.0**

THE TRUE MEANING OF "LOVE"

Let's get started!

1. Draw a picture of you and your family doing something that makes you feel truly loved.

Use words or sentences to explain WHY this makes you feel loved:

_____

_____

_____

_____

GRADES 1 & 2

"Please answer question #1 on your Academic Focus Page." Have students share their answers after they finish. It's not necessary for you to point out the ones that are love vs. romance yet. You will be doing that in a minute when you start into the teaching/presentation section.

(Solicit several answers.) [It is a guarantee that many of the examples will be in connection with romance.]

Ask the students, **"Do you think I would be in here to teach you how to date better? How to find a boyfriend or girlfriend?** *(Laugh with the students if appropriate.)* **I can assure you that I'm not here to teach you about dating. I am, however, going to teach you seven lessons over the next seven weeks that will change your lives forever. These lessons will give you great insight into yourself and others. What I will be teaching you can be used for the rest of your life. Sound good?"** *(Rhetorical)*

TEACHING/PRESENTATION:

(Write on the white board the word "love." Explain to students that there are a number of different ways that the word love can be used in sentences (noun, adjective, etc.). Give some examples verbally. Tell them that for all of the lessons you will be teaching, love will be used as a verb or action word. Place a dash after the word "love" that you previously wrote on the board and write "verb/action word.") Say, **"For all of the lessons that I am teaching, when you hear the word 'love' I want you to immediately think that it is an action word, and you will be doing something for somebody. This is important because my lessons are going to teach you how to show and receive love. Now let's talk about the difference between love and romance."**

(Explain to the students that usually people feel uncomfortable about the word "love" because when they hear that word it reminds them of "mushy-gushy" stuff. Lots of times people decide that love must be "mushy-gushy" because on television they have seen people kissing and holding hands. After all, they are in "love" with each other.)

Say, **"How many of you have actually seen stuff like that? And how is the word love used in the sentence, 'They are in love'?** *(noun)* **But how are we using it?** *(verb)* **So you can see that there is a big difference between what we will be learning and what you may have seen on television or how other people have used the word. The stuff you see**

AFP: Lesson 1.0, Grade 5–6, #1

Name _____ Date _____ | **LESSON 1.0**

THE TRUE MEANING OF "LOVE"

Let's get started!

1. **What is your own definition of love?** (Write a sentence(s) or individual words to create your own definition.)

_____
_____
_____
_____
_____

In the definition that you wrote above, does it describe love as a verb, noun, or adjective? (Circle the one(s) that apply.)

VERB   NOUN   ADJECTIVE

2. **What makes you feel loved?** For this exercise *don't* spend a lot of time thinking about it! (Read the words and quickly place a check in two of the ovals. Draw a line from the two ovals you chose to the question mark.)

Hug

You are amazing!   **?**   Happy Birthday!

Want to hang out?   I did your chores for you.

GRADES 5 & 6

TEACHING/PRESENTATION:

1. Write the word "love" on the white board.

2. Explain the different ways that the word love can be used *(noun, verb, etc.)*.

3. Tell them that you will be using the word "love" as an action word.

4. Start discussion on the difference between love and romance.
   - **Academic Focus Page [Lesson 1.0, Grade 5–6, #2]**
   - **Academic Focus Page [Lesson 1.0, Grade 3–4, #1]**

5. Discuss the fact that there are five basic ways that people feel loved.
   - **Academic Focus Page [Lesson 1.0, Grades 3–4, #2]**

on television is something we usually call romance, and it is quite different from our definition of love. This is what makes these lessons so exciting. I'm going to be showing you a different way to look at the word "love" and how it can be used to make people's lives, including your own, a lot better. Okay, so let me ask you my next question: 'What makes you feel loved?'"

Grade 5 or 6, continue here:	Lesson 1.0, Grade 5–6, #2

"Please read silently along with me while I read the directions from exercise #2." Read directions and have students do the exercise. After they are done, have them turn to a friend and explain why they chose those two. They may not know, and that's okay. This exercise has the purpose of getting them to think in terms of why they made their choices and eventually connecting them to the love languages as the lessons proceed. Keep your focus on open discussion and know there are many ways to interpret these. For example, "Happy Birthday!" might make somebody feel good because they are being recognized by a friend with kind words OR it could conjure up the idea that they are getting a gift. Encourage thinking in relationship to the original question, "What makes you feel loved?"

(If students don't have any answers, prompt them. You are looking for answers such as, "When my mom makes my bed," or "My dad plays with me.") Then ask, **"Do you think that all people feel loved in the same way?"**

Grade 3 or 4, continue here:	Lesson 1.0, Grade 3–4, #1

"Please answer question #1 on your Academic Focus Page." Give students a chance to write their answers. Ask students to share what they have written with another student, and then ask for a few volunteers to share with the class.

(Solicit answers from students, and have them explain why or why not. The obvious answer is no, not all people feel loved in the same way.)

Then say, **"You are exactly right. People don't all feel loved in the same way. In fact, there are five basic ways that make people feel loved, and two of the five are the ways that make most people, including you, feel the most loved. These two out of the five can be different for everybody. We call these five different ways to love people the**

Name _____ Date _____

LESSON 1.0

THE TRUE MEANING OF "LOVE"

Let's get started!

1. **What is your own definition of love?** (Write a sentence(s) or individual words to create your own definition.)

_____
_____
_____
_____
_____

In the definition that you wrote above, does it describe love as a verb, noun, or adjective? (Circle the one(s) that apply.)

VERB   NOUN   ADJECTIVE

2. **What makes you feel loved?** For this exercise *don't* spend a lot of time thinking about it! (Read the words and quickly place a check in two of the ovals. Draw a line from the two ovals you chose to the question mark.)

GRADES 5 & 6

Name _____ Date _____

LESSON 1.0

THE TRUE MEANING OF "LOVE"

Let's get started!

1. **Do you think all people feel loved in the same way?** (Write a sentence or two explaining why or why not.)

_____
_____
_____
_____
_____

2. **Who makes you feel truly loved?** (In the five circles below put the names of five people who truly make you feel loved. If you can't think of five, then write as many as you can.)

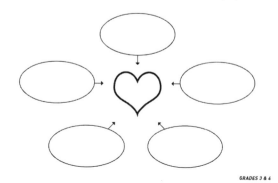

GRADES 3 & 4

'love languages.' *(Write "Love Languages" on the board.)* **Over the next six weeks, one of your jobs is to figure out which two make you feel loved. While you are trying to figure out your two love languages, you will be learning about all five love languages so you can better understand what makes other people feel loved. In the meantime, think to yourself, 'Who makes me feel loved?' "**

Grade 3 or 4, continue here:	Lesson 1.0, Grade 3–4, #2

Have students write the names of five people who make them feel truly loved. If they can't think of five, that's okay. Some children really may not have that many people who love them, and this is a great place for you or the counselor to discover a greater need in this child's life. Not having enough people in a student's life to love them creates all kinds of problems.

"Sometimes we try to love people in a language that they don't understand, and it doesn't make them feel loved at all. We think that if we like to be loved a certain way, then everybody must like to be loved that same way. But as you know now, not everyone feels loved the same way. Once you figure out what makes people feel loved, you can really be a better friend to them. Each time I come in here, I'm going to teach you about one of the love languages, so you will have to wait until next time to find out what the first one is."

CLOSURE:

1. Have students hold thumbs up or down if they agree that the word "love" is going to be used as a verb/action word. *(Thumbs should be up in agreement that it is going to be used as a verb/action word.)*

2. Have a couple of students share with the class the difference between love and romance as it relates to the lessons you are going to teach. *(Love is an action word, which means we are going to be doing something for someone, as opposed to romance, which is how we feel toward someone.)*

3. Have the class hold up their hands and indicate with their fingers how many basic ways there are to love people. *(Five)*

4. Have students repeat the learning objective on the white board and discuss how well they learned it.

AFP: Lesson 1.0, Grade 3–4, #2

Name _____ Date _____ | **LESSON 1.0**

THE TRUE MEANING OF "LOVE"

Let's get started!

1. **Do you think all people feel loved in the same way?** (Write a sentence or two explaining why or why not.)

_____

_____

_____

_____

_____

2. **Who makes you feel truly loved?** (In the five circles below put the names of five people who truly make you feel loved. If you can't think of five, then write as many as you can.)

GRADES 3 & 4

CLOSURE:

1. Have students hold thumbs up or down if they agree that the word "love" is going to be used as a verb/action word. *(Thumbs should be up in agreement that it is going to be used as a verb/action word.)*

2. Have a couple of students share with the class the difference between love and romance as it relates to the lessons you are going to teach. *(Love is an action word that means we are going to be doing something for someone, as opposed to romance, which is how we feel toward someone.)*

3. Have the class hold up their hands and indicate with their fingers how many basic ways you are going to teach them how to love people. *(Five)*

4. Have students repeat the learning objective on the white board and discuss how well they learned it.

CHAPTER 3
Words of Affirmation

INTRODUCTION

The first love language I taught was Words of Affirmation. It seemed fitting for a couple of reasons. 1. It's something that everyone can relate to, and 2. It's the most overused love language available. Let's face it, we all know that giving praise is very important, and in the academic world, its emphasis is everywhere. On any given day, in any given school, you will see posters, smiley faces, positive power sayings, quotes of the day, and affirmations galore given out by educators. So when I say, "This is the one everyone can relate to," it doesn't necessarily mean this is the one that is done well.

We as educators typically use what I like to call the shotgun approach. This is where we go around praising and over-praising with the effect of reaching some children while believing that we are reaching all children. It is true that children are encouraged through positive words whether it's their language or not, but it is not true that all children will benefit as much as others from Words of Affirmation. Remember, one primary emphasis of this book is to teach you and your students how to discover who feels loved by each of the love languages, including positive praise. I'm in no way trying to discourage you from using the "shotgun approach" because it's better than nothing, and it's also a good way to find out who benefits the most from those wonderful words of encouragement. On the other hand my goal here, as with all the love languages, is for you to discover and become an expert at identifying the ways that you and others feel loved in a very meaningful way. Again, I'm not against the "shotgun approach" because it's important to praise all students whether it's their love language or not. When we discover children's specific love languages, that doesn't mean we don't ever do any of the others for them. All people generally like any kindness extended to them, even if it's not their love language.

LESSON 2
Words of Affirmation
(SCRIPTED)

OBJECTIVE:

Students will be introduced to the first love language *(Words of Affirmation)*, and will be able to describe what it is and how to use it. They will also be able to identify the opposite of this love language as *(harassment)*. Students will be able to understand reporting procedures, school rules, and the devastating effect harassment has on people. Further, students will understand what flattery is and why using it creates lack of trust.

On the white board write:

1. I can describe to someone what Words of Affirmation are.
2. I can tell someone what harassment is and how to report it.
3. I can describe flattery to someone and why it creates lack of trust.

(Have students talk with each other for thirty seconds about what they think they are going to be learning today.)

REVIEW:

Instructor will go over the previous lesson by asking volunteer students to explain:

1. Review the last lesson's objectives that you wrote on the white board.
2. What is the first thing that we want you to think of when you hear the word "love"? *(It is being used as a verb/action word for these lessons, and that means we will be doing something for or to someone.)*
3. What is the difference between love and romance?

ANTICIPATORY SET:

Today we will be learning about the first love language. It is called Words of Affirmation. *(Have entire class say the love language together and write "Words of Affirmation" on the board.)* **An affirmation is something said or written that speaks to the**

LESSON 2
Words of Affirmation
(ABBREVIATED)

OBJECTIVE:

Students will be introduced to the first love language *(Words of Affirmation)*, and will be able to describe what it is and how to use it. They will be able to identify the opposite of this love language as *(harassment)*. Students will be able to understand reporting procedures, school rules, and the devastating effect harassment has on people. Further, students will understand what flattery is and why using it creates lack of trust.

On the white board write:

1. I can describe to someone what Words of Affirmation are.
2. I can tell someone what harassment is and how to report it.
3. I can describe flattery to someone and why it creates lack of trust.

(Have students talk with each other for thirty seconds about what they think they are going to be learning today.)

REVIEW:

Instructor will go over the previous lesson by asking volunteer students to explain:

1. Review the last lesson's objectives that you wrote on the white board.
2. What is the first thing that we want you to think of when you hear the word "love"? *(It is being used as a verb/action word for these lessons, and that means we will be doing something for or to someone.)*
3. What is the difference between love and romance?

ANTICIPATORY SET:

1. Introduce the first love language "Words of Affirmation."

2. Define affirmation for the class.

existence of the truth of something. In other words, it is a way that we say nice things to people that are truthful. So "Words of Affirmation" are truthful words spoken or written from one person to another that will uplift them and can make them feel good, encouraged, or loved. *(Write "truthful words" on the board.)*

TEACHING/PRESENTATION:

Let's get started. The first thing I want to tell you about the love languages is that even though there are five of them, most people usually prefer two of the five. In other words, they usually discover that two of the five love languages are their favorites, and these two are the ones that make them feel the "most loved." Your job is to listen each week and to ask yourself, "Is the love language that I learned about today one that makes me feel good or feel loved?" Sometimes this can be very confusing, because the truth is everybody likes all five of the love languages but not all of the languages make them feel loved. The purpose of my teaching you these languages is twofold: 1. So that you can figure out what makes you feel loved. 2. So that you can be able to figure out what makes other people feel loved. *(Write on the board: "To figure out what makes you feel loved and what makes others feel loved.")*

As I said before, Words of Affirmation are truthful words that encourage people. Sometimes, but not always, Words of Affirmation can be compliments. There are some words of affirmation like "I love you" that are words of affirmation but not necessarily a compliment. Give me some examples of words that you have heard that made you feel good or encouraged. *(Write some of the examples that students say on the board.)*

There are many ways to encourage people with words. Sometimes we can write words that make people feel good, for example in cards or letters. So Words of Affirmation aren't just said; they can be written as well.

Grade 1 or 2, continue here:	Lesson 2.0, Grade 1–2, #1

Read directions to students and have them fill in the ovals with five encouraging words that they can use in sentences. Depending on the ability of your students, they can either make up their own words or copy the ones that you wrote on the board. Again, remember that this Academic Focus Page has been created for two different grade levels. A first grade student may be expected to do only one or two sentences while a second grade student would do all five.

3. Write "Truthful Words" on the board.

TEACHING/PRESENTATION:

1. Explain how people prefer two of the five *(typically)*.

2. Explain that their job is to figure out which two love languages make them feel loved.

3. Explain your two goals for teaching these lessons.
   a. That they can figure out their own love language.
   b. To figure out what makes other people feel loved.

4. Have students describe words that they have heard that make them feel loved.

5. Explain that Words of Affirmation include written words.
   • **Academic Focus Page [Lesson 2.0, Grade 1–2, #1]**
   • **Academic Focus Page [Lesson 2.0, Grade 3–4, #1]**
   • **Academic Focus Page [Lesson 2.0, Grade 5–6, #1]**

AFP: Lesson 2.0, Grade 1–2, #1

Name _____ Date _____ **LESSON 2.0**

WORDS OF AFFIRMATION
○ *Makes me feel loved.*
○ *I like it.*

1. **Words of Affirmation** are truthful words that are spoken or written from one person to another that will uplift them and can make them feel good, encouraged, or loved. Think of five words that you could use in a sentence that would make people feel good, encouraged, or loved and write them in the bubbles. An example has been done for you!

great

1.

5.

2.

4.

3.

Use each word that you wrote above in a sentence to make someone feel good.
*Example: You are a **great** friend!*

1. _____

2. _____

3. _____

4. _____

5. _____

GRADES 1 & 2

| Grade 3 or 4, continue here: | Lesson 2.0, Grade 3–4, #1 |

We are now going to do exercise number 1 on your 2.0 lesson. Follow along silently as I read the directions to you. Have students write sentences, and then call on a few students to share their answers with the rest of the class.

| Grade 5 or 6, continue here: | Lesson 2.0, Grade 5–6, #1 |

We are now going to do exercise number 1 on your 2.0 lesson. Follow along silently as I read the directions to you. Have students fill in the boxes with Words of Affirmation in one box and symbols in another. When the students have completed this exercise, have them come up to the white board (two at a time) and write one word or draw one symbol. Have all students continue to do this until there are no new ideas. Invite students to discuss why they wrote their word or drew the symbol. *[Symbols are a non-linguistic representation that can be a very powerful and an often overlooked way for students to express themselves.]*

Now we are going to do an exercise that I call the "Fakey Lesson" to show you how powerful words can be.

EXERCISE:

1. Have the students pair up. If there are an odd number of students, pair the odd student up with the teacher.
2. Have one student from each of the pairs raise their hand.
3. Tell the students that the student with their hand raised will go first.
4. Tell the students who had their hand raised to say to their partner what you are about to say, which is, **"You're really cool."**
5. Without failure, the students are going to say this without much emotion, and I always tell my students that they sound like a bunch of moaning cows. Demonstrate for them what you see with another student. Have them try it again, only this time you say, "You're really cool!" with some excitement in your voice. Have the same students try it again and repeat after you.
6. Reverse this and have the other students say the same thing back to the first students.
7. Now tell the students who had their hand raised to say to their partner what you are about to say, which is, **"I'm really glad you're in my class!"**

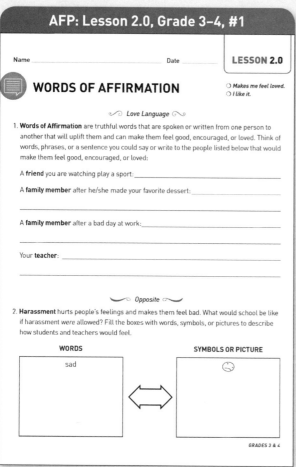

AFP: Lesson 2.0, Grade 3–4, #1

Name _____ Date _____   **LESSON 2.0**

💬 WORDS OF AFFIRMATION

○ *Makes me feel loved.*
○ *I like it.*

〜 *Love Language* 〜

1. **Words of Affirmation** are truthful words that are spoken or written from one person to another that will uplift them and can make them feel good, encouraged, or loved. Think of words, phrases, or a sentence you could say or write to the people listed below that would make them feel good, encouraged, or loved:

A **friend** you are watching play a sport: _____

A **family member** after he/she made your favorite dessert: _____
_____

A **family member** after a bad day at work: _____
_____

Your **teacher**: _____
_____

〜 *Opposite* 〜

2. **Harassment** hurts people's feelings and makes them feel bad. What would school be like if harassment *were* allowed? Fill the boxes with words, symbols, or pictures to describe how students and teachers would feel.

WORDS		SYMBOLS OR PICTURE
sad	⟺	☹

GRADES 3 & 4

AFP: Lesson 2.0, Grade 5–6, #1

Name _____ Date _____   **LESSON 2.0**

💬 WORDS OF AFFIRMATION

○ *Makes me feel loved.*
○ *I like it.*

1. **Words of Affirmation** are truthful words that are spoken or written from one person to another that will uplift them and can make them feel good, encouraged, or loved. [Think of your own **Words of Affirmation** and place these words and symbols in the two boxes below. We have provided examples to get you started!]

〜 *Love Language* 〜

WORDS	SYMBOLS OR PICTURE
You are awesome!	♡

〜 *Opposite* 〜

2. **Harassment** hurts people's feelings and makes them feel bad. (In your own words, write three things that describe what you have learned about harassment.)

1. _____
2. _____
3. _____

🚫 NEGATIVE BEHAVIORS

Flattery is another example of negative behavior. People who use flattery are often NOT trusted by other people and are considered immature.

GRADES 5 & 6

---

6. Exercise: Fakey Lesson

7. Put closure on the Fakey Lesson.

8. Transition to [Part 2] of lesson.

8. Have their partners say the same thing back to them.

9. Have students sit down.

(When you finish this exercise, you should be able to observe a classroom full of students who are laughing, smiling, and somewhat excited. It is human nature to feel good when people are saying nice things to each other. Discuss this fact with the students, and remind them that if this exercise makes them feel good and it is fake/not real, imagine how good it makes people feel when they say nice things and really mean it. Words of Affirmation are truthful words that encourage people. Let them know that it would be nice if they always used words to encourage people, but unfortunately, some students use words in a negative way. Transition the students to hear about the opposite of Words of Affirmation.)

[TRANSITION TO OPPOSITE]

ANTICIPATORY SET:

There are opposites to everything. All of the love languages that I'm going to teach you have an opposite as well. The opposite of the love language describes negative behavior. When we say nice things to people, we make them feel good, uplifted, encouraged, and loved. This is the positive side of the love language of "Words of Affirmation," and when we say negative things to people, this would be considered the negative side or opposite of this love language. Does everyone understand? *(check for understanding)*

Grade 1 or 2, continue here:	Lesson 2.1, Grade 1–2, #1

Have students locate octagon #1 on their Academic Focus Page. Point to the word "Harassment" and have the students do the same. Say the word out loud for the class to hear. Have the students practice saying the word with you. Ask the students if they have heard this word before then have them circle yes or no. Read the definition to them and have them read the definition with you as a class.

TEACHING/PRESENTATION:

The opposite of a love language never makes people feel good, and in fact, it always has the potential to hurt people. The opposite of "Words of Affirmation" is when hurtful words are said to a person. We call these words put-downs because they put people down. You may have heard this kind of talk at school when kids get angry, like, "You're stupid" or "You can't do anything right!" Our school takes this type of talk very

[TRANSITION TO OPPOSITE]

ANTICIPATORY SET:

1. Discuss that there are many things that have opposites, and this includes all five of the love languages.

   Positive side = Good

   Negative side = Bad

2. **Academic Focus Page [Lesson 2.1, Grade 1–2, #1]**

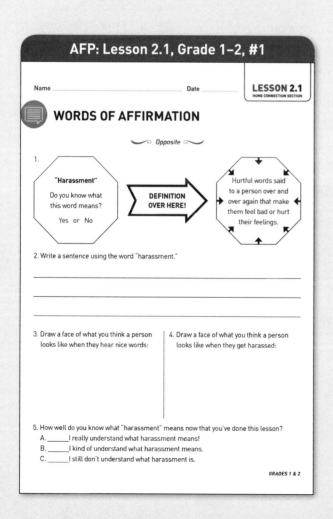

seriously. We actually have rules that don't allow students to talk to each other like that.

When one person or a group of people continues to call another person names and keeps putting them down over and over again, we call this harassment. Harassment is against our school rules. *[Insert whatever your school policy/discipline procedures are here if you like.]*

Our government takes harassment very seriously as well. According to the law, harassment can include a lot more things than just saying mean things. It can also include: physically harming another student or their property, interfering with a student's education, creating a threatening educational environment, disrupting the orderly conduct of the school, making a threatening phone call, or sending a threatening text/email.

We want all of our students to feel safe, and this includes not being harassed by other students. If you are being harassed or know someone who is being harassed, we want you to tell someone. *[Insert whatever your school procedure is for reporting harassment.]*

Grade 1 or 2, continue here: Lesson 2.1, Grade 1–2, #2, #3, #4 & #5

Have students locate box #2. Reread the example of harassment and have them write a sentence using the word "harassment." They can then proceed to draw pictures in #3 and #4 to help them understand the word. Have a classroom discussion about times when they have felt harassed. When you are finished with the discussion, have students "self-assess" by circling one of the responses at the bottom right-hand side of the page. Read each of the choices to the students. You can do this as a whole group or you can choose to sit with each child individually, which would give you the opportunity to reteach the concept if needed. Either way, students should have the opportunity for clarification if needed. Have student do the self-assess again after they have gained more clarification.

TEACHING/PRESENTATION:

1. Opposites of love languages never make people feel good and always have the potential to hurt someone.

2. Discuss put-downs.

3. Introduce the definition of harassment.

4. Discuss school policy regarding harassment.

5. Discuss reporting procedures if student is harassed or sees someone else being harassed.

6. Discuss government laws regarding harrassment.
   - **Academic Focus Page [Lesson 2.1, Grade 1–2, #2 & #3]**
   - **Academic Focus Page [Lesson 2.0, Grade 3–4, #2]**
   - **Academic Focus Page [Lesson 2.0, Grade 5–6, #2]**

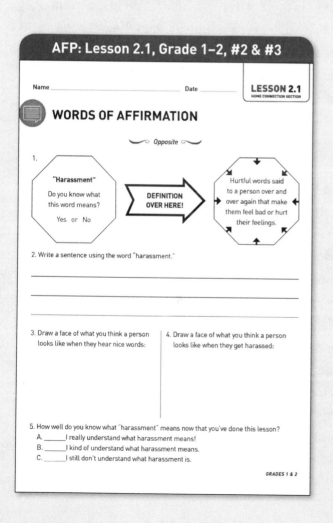

AFP: Lesson 2.1, Grade 1–2, #2 & #3

Name _____ Date _____

LESSON 2.1
HOME CONNECTION SECTION

WORDS OF AFFIRMATION

~ Opposite ~

1.

"Harassment"

Do you know what this word means?

Yes or No

DEFINITION OVER HERE!

Hurtful words said to a person over and over again that make them feel bad or hurt their feelings.

2. Write a sentence using the word "harassment."

_____

_____

3. Draw a face of what you think a person looks like when they hear nice words:

4. Draw a face of what you think a person looks like when they get harassed:

5. How well do you know what "harassment" means now that you've done this lesson?
   A. _____ I really understand what harassment means!
   B. _____ I kind of understand what harassment means.
   C. _____ I still don't understand what harassment is.

GRADES 1 & 2

Grade 3 or 4, continue here: Lesson 2.0, Grade 3–4, #2

We are now going to do exercise number 1 on your 2.0 lesson. Follow along silently as I read the directions to you. Have students write words and symbols to describe what school would be like for students and teachers if harassment *were* allowed.

 When students are done with this activity, have them share their answers with a partner. Have individual students volunteer answers and have a whole group discussion. Allow the students to explain what the school would be like, and if you prefer, you can go deeper by asking them what the United States would be like if it were allowed. After you are done with the discussion, ask them the rhetorical question, **"Aren't you glad that there are laws against harassment?"**

Grade 5 or 6, continue here: Lesson 2.0, Grade 5–6, #2

We are now going to do exercise number 2 on your 2.0 lesson. Follow along silently as I read the directions to you. Read the directions, and have them write three things that they learned about harassment. Have students talk to a partner about what they learned. Ask individual students to volunteer what they learned with the class. When they are done talking about harassment, have a student read the definition of flattery at the bottom of the page and hold a classroom discussion regarding why people who use flattery are often not trusted and thought of as immature.

Another area that we need to talk about that isn't against the law, but is considered a negative behavior, is called flattery. Flattery is when you tell someone something nice so that you can get something for yourself. Now I'm sure none of you have ever done this before! *(sarcasm) (Students will usually snicker because they know they do this with lots of different people. Remind students that when they do this, it's obvious to the people they are doing it too. I usually role-play an example like, "Mom, you are the best mom ever! Can I go over to my friend's house?")* **Using Words of Affirmation to get something is wrong. You can usually tell if you are flattering someone because after you give them a compliment or say something nice it is followed with questions such as, "Can I have . . ." or "Can I go . . ." When people use flattery to get things for themselves, it destroys trust. The person who is being flattered realizes that you aren't being honest with your words, and they become suspicious of you. They start to wonder if they can trust the things that you say. Most people don't like to be friends with flatterers.**

AFP: Lesson 2.0, Grade 3–4, #2

Name _____ Date _____

LESSON 2.0

WORDS OF AFFIRMATION

○ *Makes me feel loved.*
○ *I like it.*

⌒〜 Love Language 〜⌒

1. **Words of Affirmation** are truthful words that are spoken or written from one person to another that will uplift them and can make them feel good, encouraged, or loved. Think of words, phrases, or a sentence you could say or write to the people listed below that would make them feel good, encouraged, or loved:

A **friend** you are watching play a sport: _____

A **family member** after he/she made your favorite dessert: _____
_____

A **family member** after a bad day at work: _____
_____

Your **teacher**: _____
_____

〜⌒ Opposite ⌒〜

2. **Harassment** hurts people's feelings and makes them feel bad. What would school be like if harassment *were* allowed? Fill the boxes with words, symbols, or pictures to describe how students and teachers would feel.

WORDS		SYMBOLS OR PICTURE
sad	⟷	☹

GRADES 3 & 4

AFP: Lesson 2.0, Grade 5–6, #2

Name _____ Date _____

LESSON 2.0

WORDS OF AFFIRMATION

○ *Makes me feel loved.*
○ *I like it.*

1. **Words of Affirmation** are truthful words that are spoken or written from one person to another that will uplift them and can make them feel good, encouraged, or loved. (Think of your own **Words of Affirmation** and place these words and symbols in the two boxes below. We have provided examples to get you started!)

⌒〜 Love Language 〜⌒

WORDS	SYMBOLS OR PICTURE
You are awesome!	♡

〜⌒ Opposite ⌒〜

2. **Harassment** hurts people's feelings and makes them feel bad. (In your own words, write three things that describe what you have learned about harassment.)

1. _____
2. _____
3. _____

🚫 NEGATIVE BEHAVIORS

Flattery is another example of negative behavior. People who use flattery are often NOT trusted by other people and are considered immature.

GRADES 5 & 6

7. Introduce the concept of flattery.

8. Discuss the harmful results of flattery.

9. Discuss the mature way to deal with things when making a request of another person.
   • **Academic Focus Page [Lesson 2.0, Grade 5–6, #2]**

When you want something, you should ask for it straightforwardly and honestly. If the person doesn't want to give you something or do something that you requested, be ready to accept their answer. In other words, if the answer is "no," then it's "no." Rather than argue over their answer, just ask if there would be another time that you could get whatever it is you want. Growing up and becoming mature means that you are able to accept someone else's answer even if it's not the one you want to hear.

Grade 5 or 6, continue here:	Lesson 2.0, Grade 5–6, #2

Have students look at the bottom of the Academic Focus Page. Ask an individual student to read the definition of flattery and hold a classroom discussion regarding why people who use flattery are often not trusted and thought of as immature.

Okay, now let's go over the things that we have learned today.

CLOSURE:

Today we learned about the love language called Words of Affirmation. We learned that Words of Affirmation are truthful words (spoken or written) that can include compliments that build up and encourage people. We also learned that every love language has an opposite. Two negative behaviors that we learned about today are harassment or saying things to people that are hurtful, and flattery, which is saying nice things in order to selfishly get something for ourselves.

What are my two goals for you whenever I teach the love languages? *(Call on students: 1. to learn your own love language, and 2. to be able to figure out what the love languages of others are.)* Ask yourself today, "Do Words of Affirmation make me feel loved?" Or, "Even though I like to hear kind words, do they make me feel loved?" Please fill in a circle by one of the items at the top right-hand side of your Academic Focus Page. The items say, "Makes me feel loved," or "I like it."

The best way to learn the love languages is to use them. Try to think of people that you know who may really feel loved when you say kind words to them. I'm going to give you a very simple assignment. When you do this assignment, I want you to remember how it went and be ready to report to the class. When I teach the next lesson, I'm going to call on a few people to see what kind of experience they had. Here is the assignment:

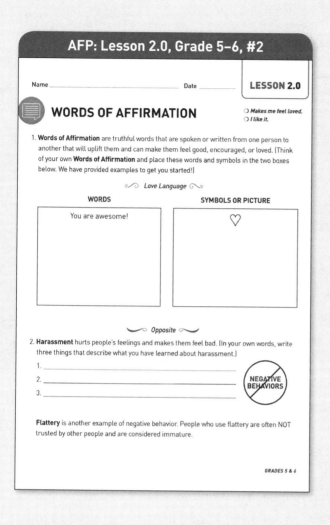

CLOSURE:

1. Go over definition of **Words of Affirmation**.

2. Restate the two negative behaviors:
   a. Harassment
   b. Flattery

3. Have students restate your goals for teaching them the love languages:
   a. to learn their own love language
   b. to be able to figure out what other people's love languages are

4. Please fill in a circle by one of the items at the top right-hand side of your Academic Focus Page. The items say, "Makes me feel loved," or "I like it."

5. Give instructions for the independent practice.

INDEPENDENT PRACTICE/ASSIGNMENT:

1. Have each student say at least one nice thing to a student who isn't currently in their classroom. The thing that they say needs to be truthful, unexpected, and meant to encourage the other person.

2. Have each student say something nice to their mom or dad that is truthful, unexpected, and meant to encourage them. Encourage them to tell their parents that they love them if this is something that they don't normally do and especially if they have never done it. *[I understand this may not be appropriate for all students. Have them say it if they are comfortable. There are some situations where a child shouldn't be forced to say "I love you" to their parent if they don't feel that way. Let them be the judge of who in the family they will compliment. The majority of home situations will be fine for the student to say "I love you." This book is written for the majority of students. I have every confidence that you will adjust where/when needed.]*

3. Remind the students that they don't need to explain to people that this is for an assignment. I ask the students, What would it sound like if I went up to someone and said, "This is an assignment, so I just wanted to say I really like the way you play baseball"? I explain to them that if they tell people it's an assignment, then that person won't feel that they are being sincere or honest about what they are saying. It would be like having your mom or dad come up to you and say, "I'm your parent, so I'm going to say I love you because it's my job. I love you . . ." Students usually laugh and get the point.

4. Ask students to give examples again of things they could say to different people. Encourage them to be very specific in their words. "I really like that blue shirt on you; it looks really awesome!" Instead of, "You look nice."

5. Remind students that because many of them rarely compliment their family members, they may be suspicious of their motives. I have had a number of students who have come back and reported that the first thing their parents say after they give them a compliment, is "What do you want?" If that happens to a student, tell them it's okay to explain to their parents that they are practicing Words of Affirmation.

6. Tell students when you will return for the next lesson and when to have their assignment completed.

7. Review the objectives from white board. Have students talk for a few seconds about how well they learned the three objectives.

INDEPENDENT PRACTICE/ASSIGNMENT:

1. Have students use Words of Affirmation by:

    a. giving a compliment to a student who isn't in the classroom.

    b. giving a compliment to their father or mother.

2. Remind students that they don't need to explain to people that this is an assignment, and explain why.

3. Tell students that you will be asking them about their assignment experience next time you teach about the love languages.

4. Tell students what day you are planning on teaching them the next love language lesson.

5. Review the objectives from white board. Have students talk for a few seconds about how well they learned the three objectives that you set.

LESSON

2

Words of Affirmation

ABBREVIATED

FINAL THOUGHTS

Kids can be brutal to one another. There are hurtful things said at school every day. Arming our students with the ability to identify harassment and being able to report it is very important. Reporting looks quite different from tattling. I tell students that tattling is for the purpose of getting someone in trouble. I usually teach students how to identify the difference between reporting and tattling in a separate lesson if the teacher hasn't already done so. Most teachers go over these differences for their own sanity.

Sometimes when I'm teaching about this negative behavior, I start by saying the poem, "sticks and stones may break my bones but . . ." and have the students finish the rest of it. After they finish the poem I say, "This poem is a lie. Words can and do hurt. Sometimes they hurt worse than physical actions." I tell the students that words leave the mouth, go into the ears, and straight to the heart. Once people say something, it can never be taken back. They can ask someone to forgive them for what they said, but it won't take the words away. Then I tell them to be very, very careful about what they say.

Another thought about the assignment is to give rewards for students who participate when you call on them. Let students know that you will be calling on different people each week to see how their assignment went. If they get called on they will receive a ticket into a drawing for a prize at the end of the lesson. I find that raffle drawing tickets are great. I hand them to the student when they volunteer and have them write their names on it. When all of the love language lessons are complete, I have a final drawing for the prizes.

We as educators are usually pretty good at praising our students. If we aren't, then students won't like to be in our classroom even if it **isn't** their love language. Practice giving students specific compliments, and through these lessons, identify the ones who feel loved by Words of Affirmation. When we discover our students' love languages and start loving them in the way that fits best, then they will be much more likely to work toward their academic goals. This connection between instructor and student is crucial for educational excellence.

FROM THE CLASSROOM

After I taught this lesson, I went back into the same classroom a week later to teach the next love language. I asked the students how the assignment went *(something that I do before I teach each love language)*. A fourth grade girl, who came from a rough home life, raised her hand, and I asked how it went.

She said in a quiet voice, "I told my mom that I loved her."

I said, "Great! Was that the first time you ever told her that?"

"Yes," she said quietly.

And I said, "What was her reaction?"

She said, "She started crying, gave me a big hug, and didn't let go for a long time."

I said, "Do you think that is her love language?"

She said, "Yeah, and she told me that she loved me too. That's the first time I ever heard my mom tell me that she loved me, and we both were crying."

I looked at her face, and her eyes were slightly teary. "Thank you for taking this assignment seriously and really trying. That means a lot to me. I hope you and your mom will be able to say a lot more nice things to each other."

It amazes me that we still have homes where parents and children never verbalize their love for one another. The lesson I learned on this day was: Never underestimate these assignments. So many doors are opened through the simplest of actions.

CHAPTER 4

Quality Time

INTRODUCTION

Quality Time is one of my favorite love languages. I suppose I feel this way because it happens to be my primary love language. Nothing speaks love to me more than a person who is genuinely interested in my life and is willing to sacrifice their own time to be with me. Having said this, I will also say that it is hard to find people who truly know how to spend Quality Time with someone. Loving a Quality Time person takes a tremendous amount of effort.

During my observations over the years as an educator, I have discovered that a few students seem to have an intrinsic understanding of how to love people with Quality Time. Not surprisingly, these students tend to be highly sought after as friends. Though a few students come by these skills naturally, all students have the ability to learn them. When we teach students how to love people with Quality Time, we are helping them open all kinds of doorways to friendship.

Of all the love languages, Quality Time can be the most challenging for educators. First, there are many students and only one teacher! Second, the students who truly need Quality Time tend to need a lot of it! These students can usually be identified in the first week of school. They are the ones who are constantly at the teacher's desk for help, raising their hand to share a story, going to the health room, or staying in at recess. To make things even worse, Quality Time students like to be heard, and being heard often means everyone talks at once. Each one of them vying to share his or her own story!

Of course, when educators have the opportunity to work with Quality Time students, they do have a few useless options (1–7):

1. They can intimidate them into being compliant. I call this the "I'm bigger and meaner" strategy.
2. They can ignore them and hope that they will go away.
3. They can have endless discussions about following the rules.

4. They can have them sit in the hallway or another place.

5. They can go for an early retirement or seek different employment.

6. They can devote all of their attention to the Quality Time children and let everyone else fend for themselves.

7. They can do 1–6 all at the same time and any other things I couldn't think of.
   OR

8. They can teach the students about Quality Time and help them discover what motivates them to do what they do.

When teachers and students are able to communicate on deeper levels, students typically become more compliant and willing to assist the teacher. Why does this happen? It happens because the students feel more secure in the fact that the teacher knows and understands them.

Most students are constantly looking for attention because they don't feel like their needs are being met. Even if you give these students all of the Quality Time in the world, it will still never be enough. In order for the Quality Time that you give them to be enough, it must be married with understanding. Quality Time students will only feel satisfied when they know that the time they are being given is intentional and deliberate. In order for this to happen, they need to know that the teacher recognizes their needs and is intentionally trying to meet them. On the other hand, it is crucial for the students to understand their needs so that both the teacher and the students are talking about the same thing. Students who understand what makes them feel loved will be able to express more clearly what they need. This is a very important concept and one of the main themes that runs throughout the love language lessons. When students are able to express their needs to teachers, both the teachers and the students have a common ground to create solutions. This basic principle holds true for all of the love languages. Believe me when I say that feeling loved or unloved has a direct correlation to student behavior!

In my school I conducted a survey that involved over 600 students from first through fifth grade. Many of us predicted that the number-one love language chosen by our students would be gifts. To our surprise, it was overwhelmingly Quality Time, with gifts at the bottom of the list. Is this any wonder? Think about how many moms and dads have to work just to get by, how many teachers are being given more responsibilities, and how many family constellations are spread across America. Children are starving for Quality Time, and their behaviors are showing it at school. Let's educate our students to understand their needs, that they may address them with their families, educators, and friends. Let's have open and honest discussions about what makes people feel loved and bring this basic human element back into our schools. Together, we as educators, along with our students, can make plans to reduce behavior issues. When everyone understands, everyone wins.

LESSON 3
QUALITY TIME
(SCRIPTED)

OBJECTIVE:

Students will be introduced to the second love language (Quality Time) and will be able to describe the four Quality Time techniques and how to use them. They will also be able to describe the opposite of Quality Time, which is intentionally leaving others out, and describe alternative ways to make others feel comfortable even when they aren't able to include them.

On the white board, write:

1. I can describe Quality Time and the four techniques for demonstrating it.
2. I can describe the opposite of Quality Time.
3. I know how to make others feel comfortable even when I am not able to include them.

(Have students talk with each other for thirty seconds about what they think they are going to be learning today.)

REVIEW:

Instructor will go over the previous lesson by asking volunteer students to explain:

1. What are the two goals for teaching the love languages? *(To learn your own love languages and to be able to identify the love languages of others.)*
2. What was the last love language that was taught? *(Words of Affirmation)*
3. Review the last lesson's objectives that you wrote on the white board.
4. What are Words of Affirmation? *(Truthful words said or written to someone that encourages or uplifts them.)*
5. Name some words that we can use to encourage and uplift others. *(answers vary)*
6. What two areas are considered the opposite of Words of Affirmation? *(harassment and flattery)*
7. What are the reporting procedures if you are being harassed or witness someone else being harassed? *(Answers vary and depend on your school's policies.)*

LESSON 3
QUALITY TIME
(ABBREVIATED)

OBJECTIVE:

Students will be introduced to the second love language (Quality Time) and will be able to describe the four Quality Time techniques and how to use them. They will also be able to describe the opposite of Quality Time, which is intentionally leaving others out, and describe alternative ways to make others feel comfortable even when they aren't able to include them.

On the white board, write:

1. I can describe Quality Time and the four techniques for demonstrating it.
2. I can describe the opposite of Quality Time.
3. I know how to make others feel comfortable even when I am not able to include them.

(Have students talk with each other for thirty seconds about what they think they are going to be learning today.)

REVIEW:

Instructor will go over the previous lesson by asking volunteer students to explain:

1. What are the two goals for teaching the love languages? *(To learn your own love languages and to be able to identify the love languages of others.)*
2. What was the last love language that was taught? *(Words of Affirmation)*
3. Review the last lesson's objectives that you wrote on the white board.
4. What are Words of Affirmation? *(Truthful words said or written to someone that encourages or uplifts them.)*
5. Name some words that we can use to encourage and uplift others. *(answers vary)*
6. What two areas are considered the opposite of Words of Affirmation? *(harassment and flattery)*
7. What are the reporting procedures if you are being harassed or witness someone else being harassed? *(Answers vary and depend on your school's policies.)*

8. Call on a few volunteer students to quickly discuss how their assignment went and what they experienced.

9. Remind students that each time they learn a love language you want them to ask themselves: Does this love language make me feel loved or do I just like it?

ANTICIPATORY SET:

Today we will be learning about the second love language called Quality Time. *(Write "Quality Time" on the board.)* **Quality Time is intentional and deliberate time spent with a person to make them feel loved.** *(Write the words "intentional and deliberate" on the board.)*

Grade 5 or 6, continue here:	Lesson 3.0, Grade 5–6, #1
Have students write "intentional and deliberate" in spaces provided on Academic Focus Page.	

In other words, it's all about the person you are spending time with. Let me explain.

TEACHING/PRESENTATION:

Some people feel loved when you spend time with them. Remember, everybody likes to spend time with somebody, but not all people feel loved when they do. Quality time is more than just hanging out with someone or playing with them. It can be considered Quality Time only if you are doing it for the reason of making them feel loved. Like I wrote on the board, Quality Time is intentional and deliberate.

When you are trying to love someone with quality time, you are intentionally and deliberately being around them to make them feel loved by giving them your time. So how does this work?

Grade 5 or 6, continue here:	Lesson 3.0, Grade 5–6, #2
Have students fill in the left-hand column of their Academic Focus Page with the four quality time techniques as you teach/write them on the board.	

1. **If you have figured out that someone's love language is Quality Time, invite them to hang out with you, or ask if you can hang out with them. Quality Time people loved to be invited!** *(Write on the board, "Invite them.")*

8. Call on a few volunteer students to quickly discuss how their assignment went and what they experienced.

9. Remind students that each time they learn a love language you want them to ask themselves: Does this love language make me feel loved or do I just like it?

ANTICIPATORY SET:

1. Introduce the love language of Quality Time.

2. Write on the board that Quality Time is deliberate and intentional.
   • **Academic Focus Page [Lesson 3.0, Grade 5–6, #1]**

TEACHING/PRESENTATION:

1. Quality Time is deliberate and intentional.
   • **Academic Focus Page [Lesson 3.0, Grade 5–6, #2]**

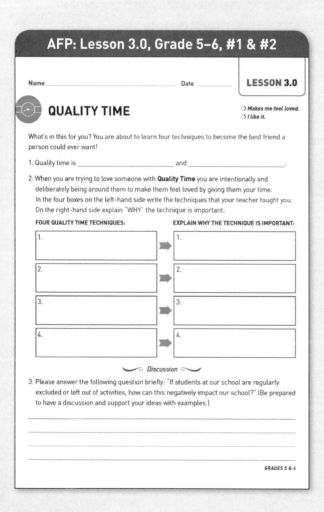

AFP: Lesson 3.0, Grade 5–6, #1 & #2

Name _____ Date _____ **LESSON 3.0**

QUALITY TIME

○ *Makes me feel loved.*
○ *I like it.*

What's in this for you? You are about to learn four techniques to become the best friend a person could ever want!

1. Quality time is _____ and _____.

2. When you are trying to love someone with **Quality Time** you are intentionally and deliberately being around them to make them feel loved by giving them your time.
   In the four boxes on the left-hand side write the techniques that your teacher taught you. On the right-hand side explain "WHY" the technique is important:

FOUR QUALITY TIME TECHNIQUES: **EXPLAIN WHY THE TECHNIQUE IS IMPORTANT:**

1. [   ] → 1. [   ]

2. [   ] → 2. [   ]

3. [   ] → 3. [   ]

4. [   ] → 4. [   ]

⸻ Discussion ⸻

3. Please answer the following question briefly: "If students at our school are regularly excluded or left out of activities, how can this negatively impact our school?" (Be prepared to have a discussion and support your ideas with examples.)

_____
_____
_____
_____

GRADES 5 & 6

2. **While you are hanging out with them, ask them if they would like to do something else or different. Try not to offer any suggestions at first. Your goal is to try to get them to say what they really want to do. Spending Quality Time with someone means that it is all about them.** *(Write on the board, "Ask them what they want to do.")*

3. **While you are spending time with a Quality Time person, ask them questions about themselves and their interests. Asking questions about someone shows that you care more about them and less about yourself. Quality Time people love it when people show that they care enough to ask questions.** *(Write on the board, "Ask them questions about things they are interested in.")*

4. **Learn to be a good listener. While they are talking about themselves, ask them other questions that show you were listening to what they said like, "So you really like basketball. Do you play on a team?"** *(Write on the board, "Be a good listener.")*

Being a friend to a Quality Time person can take a lot of effort. Students who are good at using these four techniques that I listed on the board tend to have a lot of friends. Using these four techniques doesn't just work with Quality Time people, it works with virtually everyone. The difference is, quality time people will feel loved when you use these four techniques, and others will just really, really like it. This is a great way to make and keep friends. If you are a Quality Time person, you need to learn and practice these techniques as well so that you can learn to love other Quality Time people. Can you see the value in learning these skills? *(rhetorical)*

Grade 1 or 2, continue here:	Lesson 3.0, Grade 1–2, #1 & #2

Read directions to students and have them draw a picture of themselves spending Quality Time with a friend. When they have completed the picture, have them write a sentence describing what they are doing in the picture. For advanced first grade or second grade students, they can be required to write more. Have students read their description to a partner and describe what they are doing in the picture.

2. List the four basic techniques on the board:
   1. Invite them to hang out or ask if you can hang out with them.
   2. Ask them what they want to do. Try to get them to come up with an idea.
   3. Ask them questions about their life.
   4. Be a good listener.

3. Most people who master these techniques will have a lot of friends.

4. All people like to have Quality Time but not all people feel loved by it.
   • **Academic Focus Page [Lesson 3.0, Grade 1–2, #1 & #2]**
   • **Academic Focus Page [Lesson 3.0, Grade 3–4, #1]**
   • **Academic Focus Page [Lesson 3.0, Grade 5–6, #1]**

AFP: Lesson 3.0, Grade 1–2, #1

Name _____ Date _____   **LESSON 3.0**

QUALITY TIME

○ *Makes me feel loved.*
○ *I like it.*

1. Draw a picture of you spending quality time with your friend.

2. Write a sentence describing what you are doing in the picture above.

_____
_____
_____

3. Draw a picture of someone not being included with another person during an activity.

4. How do they feel being left out? _____

GRADES 1 & 2

| Grade 3 or 4, continue here: | Lesson 3.0, Grade 3–4, #1 |

"We are now going to do exercise #1 on your 3.0 lesson. Follow along silently as I read the directions to you." Have students write sentences that focus on activities they would do with their friends or family members to make them feel loved by using the Quality Time techniques. Activities should be one-on-one instead of group-focused.

| Grade 5 or 6, continue here: | Lesson 3.0, Grade 5–6, #1 |

Have students fill in the four boxes in the right-hand column, explaining why each technique is important. After they have completed filling in all boxes for #2, extend this lesson to a deeper thinking level by having them share with the class examples of what this might look like. Give them prompts to build quality time techniques such as, "You are going to your grandparents' house for dinner. You find yourself watching TV with your grandpa and suspect that his language is Quality Time. What will you say and do using the four Quality Time techniques?"

Now let's look at the opposite of this love language.

[TRANSITION TO OPPOSITE]

ANTICIPATORY SET:
Unfortunately, not everyone is good at using the four techniques that I listed on the board. In fact, some students are all about themselves. What do we call someone when they are all about themselves? *(Selfish)*

TEACHING/PRESENTATION:
When students are all about themselves, they rarely think of anyone else's needs. They usually don't listen well, they only like to do what they want to do, and they mostly talk about themselves. These students typically don't have many real friends. It's a sad situation. They can never figure out why people don't want to be their friends. If only they could learn to use the four techniques I just listed on the board, then their life would be headed in the right direction. Ask yourself in your head, "Am I the kind of person who uses the four techniques listed on the board or am I mostly about me?" If you answered "Mostly about me," then maybe it's time to start using the four Quality

AFP: Lesson 3.0, Grade 3–4, #1

Name _____ Date _____

LESSON 3.0

QUALITY TIME

○ *Makes me feel loved.*
○ *I like it.*

1. When you are trying to love someone with **Quality Time**, you are intentionally and deliberately being around them to make them feel loved by giving them your time. Pretend that you want to make someone feel loved by spending time with them. What types of quality time activities would you do with them to make them feel loved?

_____

_____

_____

_____

HOW TO HELP SOMEBODY WHO FEELS LEFT OUT
(A "HOW-TO" COMIC STRIP)

2. Nobody wants to feel left out. Imagine that you are on the playground, at the park, or in your neighborhood and you notice that there is a kid who is being left out. Create a mini-comic strip using the information that you just learned. Help other kids understand what they can do to make him/her feel included. (You can use more paper if your teacher allows it.)

GRADES 3 & 4

AFP: Lesson 3.0, Grade 5–6, #1

Name _____ Date _____

LESSON 3.0

QUALITY TIME

○ *Makes me feel loved.*
○ *I like it.*

What's in this for you? You are about to learn four techniques to become the best friend a person could ever want!

1. Quality time is _____ and _____.

2. When you are trying to love someone with **Quality Time** you are intentionally and deliberately being around them to make them feel loved by giving them your time. In the four boxes on the left-hand side write the techniques that your teacher taught you. On the right-hand side explain "WHY" the technique is important:

FOUR QUALITY TIME TECHNIQUES:		**EXPLAIN WHY THE TECHNIQUE IS IMPORTANT:**
1.	→	1.
2.	→	2.
3.	→	3.
4.	→	4.

⌐ Discussion ⌐

3. Please answer the following question briefly: "If students at our school are regularly excluded or left out of activities, how can this negatively impact our school?" (Be prepared to have a discussion and support your ideas with examples.)

_____

_____

_____

_____

GRADES 5 & 6

[TRANSITION TO OPPOSITE]

ANTICIPATORY SET:

What do we call people who are all about themselves? *(Selfish)*

TEACHING/PRESENTATION:

1. Have students ask themselves, "Am I the kind of person who is about me, or do I regularly use the four techniques that are listed on the board?"

Time techniques on the board.

The opposite of this love language is intentionally or deliberately leaving someone out or not including them. **Where are some places you see this happening?** *(Students will suggest a variety of places including: playground, home, bus, lunchroom, classroom, etc. You will be surprised at how well they know who and where other students are being left out.)* **How does it feel to be left out?** *(Answers will vary: sad, mad, angry, hurt, jealous.)* **Sometimes when students get left out they try to make others feel left out so they know how it feels. Does this really help?** *(no)*

Skits (negative behaviors demonstration):

I want to show you a couple of situations that didn't seem right to me.

(Demonstrate for the students the following two situations.)

1. *You be a girl who is playing with another girl, when out of nowhere a third girl asks to play with you. You respond to this third girl,* **"No, you can't play with me and** *(insert name)* **because today is Tuesday and we only play with you on Thursdays."** *Then break out of character and say,* **"Ouch! That doesn't feel right."** *Then say,* **"Here's another scene that I have seen before."**

2. *Set up two chairs and desks side by side so that the class can see you. Have a volunteer student hold a book in his hand and pretend it's his lunch tray. Have him stand fifteen feet away and tell him you want him to wait for thirty seconds and come over to sit down for lunch. You sit in one chair and pretend like you're eating your lunch. When the student comes over to sit down in the only other chair, put your foot on the chair and say,* **"I'm saving this for** *(insert name)*. **You can't sit here."** * Note: *Pick a student for this skit who can handle it. Don't pick someone who is constantly left out or would otherwise take it personally.* **How many of you have seen these situations?** *[Usually many students will raise their hands.]*

Grade 1 or 2, continue here:	Lesson 3.0, Grade 1–2, #3 & #4

Read directions to students and have them draw a picture of someone not being included. Have them fill in the blank for how it feels to be left out. Have students share their picture with a partner. Encourage a few students to share their picture with the class and explain how the person is feeling.

Let's talk about some other things I could have done when these students approached me.

2. Discuss with students where they have witnessed exclusions.

3. Do the two negative behaviors skits:
   - Two girls playing and a third one wants to join.
   - Saving a seat for "your friend" at the lunchroom table.
   - **Academic Focus Page [Lesson 3.0. Grade 1-2. #3 and #4]**

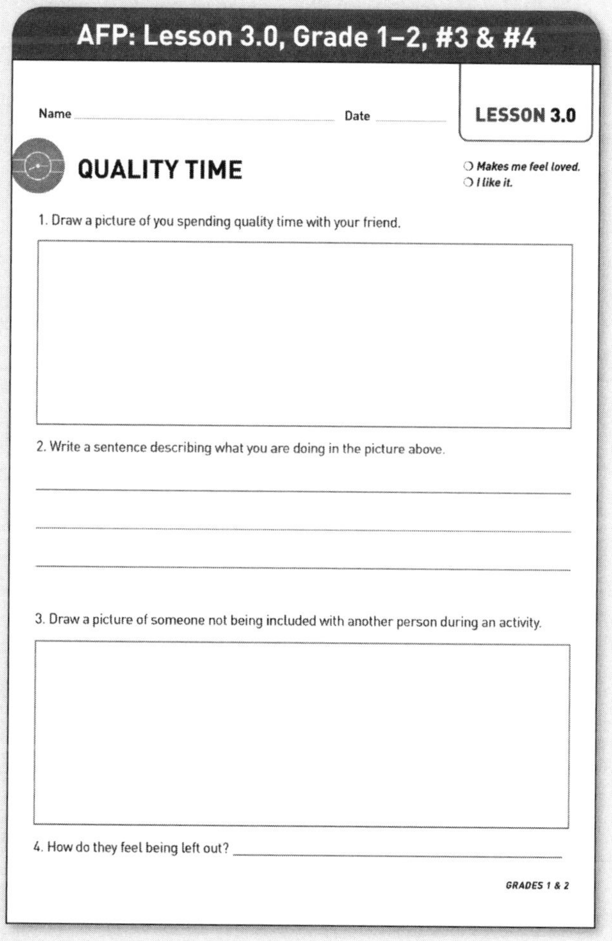

AFP: Lesson 3.0, Grade 1–2, #3 & #4

Name ____________ Date ______ LESSON 3.0

QUALITY TIME

❍ *Makes me feel loved.*
❍ *I like it.*

1. Draw a picture of you spending quality time with your friend.

2. Write a sentence describing what you are doing in the picture above.

3. Draw a picture of someone not being included with another person during an activity.

4. How do they feel being left out? ____________

GRADES 1 & 2

First, when the girl wanted to play with me I could have included her, or I could have asked her if she would have minded if we played together at a different time. I know that sometimes you may want to play with a certain friend, and that's actually okay, but making sure the person who also wants to play understands that you would like to play with them later makes it a lot better. Most people will understand this; they usually get their feelings hurt by the way things are said like, "I'm not playing with you today." Try to be very nice when you are talking to someone.

Second, everyone looks forward to going to lunch and eating with their friends. I'm going to show you a different way that I could have responded when *[insert name]* wanted to sit by me. *(Reenact the lunchroom scene with the original student. This time when the student comes over to sit down, politely tell him that you are saving this seat for (insert name), but point to a place where he or she can sit and still be near you.)* **Did you see the difference?** *(Have students state the differences.)* **When someone wants to sit by you it means that they like you. If they didn't like you, they wouldn't want to sit by you. Make sure that when you are telling them who you are saving the seat for that you don't say, "I'm saving this for my friend." If you say, "I'm saving this for my friend," what does that mean they are?** *(Students usually respond, "Not your friend," which is correct.)* **So always name the person who you are saving the seat for.**

Quality Time people and virtually everyone else want to feel included. It is our responsibility to be kind to people and make them feel included whenever it's reasonable and we can. Sometimes kids feel left out but it's not really anyone's fault. For example, sometimes kids don't get invited to a birthday party, so their feelings get hurt. But the truth is parents can only have so many kids over for their child's birthday party. Parents often tell their child that he or she can only invite five people, or something like that. So it's important to remember it's not always someone's fault. Sometimes it's out of their control.

Another place Quality Time issues can arise is out on the playground. I have seen groups of kids playing an organized game that has a certain number of people. They start playing a game like basketball and the teams are full. Some kid comes along and tries to force his way into the game. If a game is full and already in progress you should try to find something else to do rather than interrupt that game. Also, the people who are playing the game should be polite and tell the newcomer that the game is full without yelling or being mean.

Sometimes it's just not reasonable to be included or invited to everything. Try not to take it personally.

4. Go over the ways that the skits could have been done better to make the students feel included.

- It is our responsibility to include people when we can and it is reasonable.
- Most students get their feelings hurt because of the way we say things. Two examples are yelling and saying mean things.
- Sometimes we can't include people because it's out of our control:
  a. Parents set limits on birthday party.
  b. An organized game is already in progress with a preset number of players.
  c. **Academic Focus Page [Lesson 3.0, Grade 3–4, #2]**
  d. **Academic Focus Page [Lesson 3.0, Grade 5–6, #3]**

Grade 3 or 4, continue here: Lesson 3.0, Grade 3–4, #2

"We are now going to do exercise #2 on your 3.0 lesson. Follow along silently as I read the directions to you." Have students make a comic strip using the information that they just learned. The focus of this comic strip should be "How to help somebody who feels left out." Have students share their comic strip with a partner and present the comic strip to the class (if time allows). For an extended lesson you can have them do this assignment on another piece of paper and post the comic strips in the classroom or on a bulletin board. They could also share their comic strips with lower grade levels one and two.

Grade 5 or 6, continue here: Lesson 3.0, Grade 5–6, #3

"We are now going to do exercise #3 on your 3.0 lesson. Follow along silently as I read the directions to you." Have students write a couple of sentences, which will lead to a group discussion. Use the writing prompt: "If students at our school are regularly excluded or left out of activities, how can this negatively impact our school?"

CLOSURE:

Today we learned about the love language called Quality Time. Some people feel loved when you spend intentional and deliberate time with them. By inviting them to spend time with you, asking them what they want to do, asking them questions about their life, and being a good listener, you can give them the Quality Time that they need to feel loved.

Intentionally and deliberately not including people is a negative behavior, or opposite of Quality Time. Students should try to include others whenever it is reasonable and possible, even if they aren't your very best friend. When students say things in a nice way, others are a lot less likely to get their feelings hurt.

Students who are good at using the four skills to love Quality Time people usually have a lot of friends.

Ask yourself, "Does quality time make me feel loved, or do I just like it?" Please fill in a circle by one of the items at the top right-hand side of your Academic Focus Page. The items say, "Makes me feel loved," or "I like it."

AFP: Lesson 3.0, Grade 3–4, #3

Name _____ Date _____   **LESSON 3.0**

QUALITY TIME

○ *Makes me feel loved.*
○ *I like it.*

1. When you are trying to love someone with **Quality Time**, you are intentionally and deliberately being around them to make them feel loved by giving them your time. Pretend that you want to make someone feel loved by spending time with them. What types of quality time activities would you do with them to make them feel loved?

_____
_____
_____
_____

HOW TO HELP SOMEBODY WHO FEELS LEFT OUT
(A "HOW-TO" COMIC STRIP)

2. Nobody wants to feel left out. Imagine that you are on the playground, at the park, or in your neighborhood and you notice that there is a kid who is being left out. Create a mini-comic strip using the information that you just learned. Help other kids understand what they can do to make him/her feel included. (You can use more paper if your teacher allows it.)

GRADES 3 & 4

AFP: Lesson 3.0, Grade 5–6, #3

Name _____ Date _____   **LESSON 3.0**

QUALITY TIME

○ *Makes me feel loved.*
○ *I like it.*

What's in this for you? You are about to learn four techniques to become the best friend a person could ever want!

1. Quality time is _____ and _____.

2. When you are trying to love someone with **Quality Time** you are intentionally and deliberately being around them to make them feel loved by giving them your time. In the four boxes on the left-hand side write the techniques that your teacher taught you. On the right-hand side explain "WHY" the technique is important:

FOUR QUALITY TIME TECHNIQUES: → **EXPLAIN WHY THE TECHNIQUE IS IMPORTANT:**

1. → 1.
2. → 2.
3. → 3.
4. → 4.

⁓ *Discussion* ⁓

3. Please answer the following question briefly: "If students at our school are regularly excluded or left out of activities, how can this negatively impact our school?" (Be prepared to have a discussion and support your ideas with examples.)

_____
_____
_____

GRADES 5 & 6

CLOSURE:

1. Tell students the definition of Quality Time. *(deliberate and intentional)*

2. Repeat four techniques to love quality time people:
    1. Invite them to hang out or ask if you can hang out with them.
    2. Ask them what they want to do. Try to get them to come up with an idea.
    3. Ask them questions about their life.
    4. Be a good listener.

3. Deliberately and intentionally not including people is the opposite of quality time.

4. People who practice the four techniques typically have more friends.

5. Does quality time make you feel loved or do you just really like it?
    • Please fill in a circle by one of the items at the top right-hand side of your Academic Focus Page. The items say, "Makes me feel loved," or "I like it."

INDEPENDENT PRACTICE/ASSIGNMENT:

1. Have each student invite one person to join them at recess to play with them and their friends. The person they invite needs to be someone that they don't know very well, and who isn't currently in their class. This can be done as an individual or with a group of friends.

2. Remind students that it's not necessary to explain to people that this is for an assignment.

3. Ask students to give examples of things they could invite other kids to do during recess.

4. If they have a younger brother or sister, have them practice the four Quality Time techniques with them. If not, have them practice Quality Time techniques with a younger student at school during recess.

5. Tell students when you will return to teach the next lesson. Remind them that you will be asking various students about their experience the next time you teach the love languages.

6. Review the objectives from the white board. Have students discuss how well they learned the information, and answer any questions.

INDEPENDENT PRACTICE/ASSIGNMENT:

1. Have each student invite one person to join them at recess to play with them and their friends. The person they invite needs to be someone whom they don't know very well and who isn't currently in their class. This can be done as an individual or with a group of friends.
2. Remind students that they don't need to explain to people that this is for an assignment.
3. Ask students to give examples of things they could invite other kids to do during recess.
4. If they have a younger brother or sister, have them practice the four Quality Time techniques with them. If not, have them practice Quality Time techniques with a younger student at school during recess.
5. Tell students when you will return to teach the next lesson. Remind them that you will be asking various students about their experience the next time you teach the love languages.
6. Review the objectives from the white board. Have students discuss how well they learned the information and answer any questions.

FINAL THOUGHTS

As I mentioned at the beginning of this chapter, Quality Time is one of the most difficult ways for educators to love students. Time is a limited resource. I guarantee that in your school there are children who don't feel loved because there is very little or no quality time in their life. These same children show up in your school every day looking for educators and peers to fill those needs. Many times it's the behaviors of these students that drive people away, generating a vicious circle. They want Quality Time, but they don't get it, or worse, they don't think they deserve it, so they become a behavior issue and the circle is complete. The less Quality Time they get, the more unattractive and inappropriate their behavior becomes, and then people withdraw from them even more. Have you ever heard of the child who wants attention so bad that he is even willing to accept negative attention? I'm proposing that it isn't attention he seeks but rather it's Quality Time. Even though it's negative, think about the Quality Time we give to students when they get into trouble. It's all about them. Have you ever seen the most troubled student in your school become best friends with the principal, counselor, school nurse, or secretary? Think about the immense quality time those individuals have spent with that student.

When students recognize what their love languages are, they can begin to understand the needs that exist. This is a great advantage to any educator. I mentioned earlier that when the child understands and the educator understands, they can speak on the same terms. This becomes vitally important for the Quality Time child.

Once you have identified a behavior problem in your school/classroom and it's someone who happens to be a quality time student, start applying the four basic techniques on a micro level as suggested above. But before you do this, have a private discussion with the student about his or her love languages. Let them know that you understand how Quality Time makes them feel loved and that you will try to work on loving them in their language as best you can. Be honest about your limited time but tell them you think that they are important. Ask them questions about their life; be open and honest. Ask them if they feel like they are getting Quality Time at home or with their friends. Ask them how you can help. Offer the suggestion that they start seeing the school counselor to find ways to get what they need. Make sure that someone in your school is giving the child Quality Time.

School counselors can be a great benefit. Make sure that they understand the love languages. Counselors are trained to help people identify their needs and how to fill them appropriately. They usually have a few extra minutes to spend with children individually that you may not have. Let them help you and the student find realistic ways to meet these needs in the classroom and on the playground. Oftentimes behavior issues will diminish if just one adult in the school will commit to giving a child Quality Time. If you don't have a counselor, find an adult in the school who will do this. It can be virtually any school official who is willing to sit and spend just a few minutes with a child, asking him or her about their day, and so on.

As the child gets quality time with an adult, they will feel secure enough to branch out and start relating to peers. The role of the adult isn't to replace peers but to be a platform of safety from which they can reach out to peers and to which they can return when necessary. Specific conversations using the love language terms needs to happen on a regular basis.

Spending time with the child doesn't have to be lengthy. If a student's love language is Quality Time and she knows you are being intentional about meeting with her, it can be as little as three minutes. If you are lucky enough to bring a school counselor or other individual on board, it could look more like fifteen to twenty minutes a week. The most important point is that the student knows this is her time and it is intentional. In most cases, just knowing you are trying, regardless of the amount of time, goes a long way for the student. This is true for all of the love languages as the educator interacts with the students.

FROM THE CLASSROOM

After I taught the lesson on Quality Time, I had a third grade boy come to me and say, "Mr. Freed, can I meet with you?"

I said, "Sure," and we set up an appointment.

The next day this boy and I met. I asked him what was bothering him, and he told me that he felt like he never had Quality Time with his dad. When I asked him to explain, he said he had younger siblings and his parents were always busy with them. On top of that, his dad worked out of town.

He asked me if I could meet with him and his dad to explain about the love languages. I told him I would and I called his dad to set up a meeting.

The three of us met in my office and the dad seemed fairly relaxed and open to the discussion. We talked for a few minutes about his son's need for quality time and how I felt he was mature to seek out an audience with his dad. The dad listened intently and then said, "I don't understand. Just the other day we worked together in the yard." (He was being serious.) Needless to say, I went over what Quality Time looked like and we came up with a plan for him and his son to spend time together.

In the end, they drew up a schedule of the specific time they would be spending together, which didn't include the siblings. To date, the child is happy and has reported back on several occasions of the many things he and his dad have done together.

Many of the students I see have Quality Time needs. I find myself on a daily basis talking to them about their love languages. Two of my students, a fourth grade boy and a fifth grade boy, come into my office on a regular basis. Without failure they will say, "Finally, I get my quality time! This is my favorite time of the week!"

CHAPTER 5
Acts of Service

INTRODUCTION

Acts of Service can be a very confusing love language for children. On a daily basis, children receive the benefits of being children from their family. They aren't expected to earn a living, drive a car, pay the bills, or make sure that their wills are in order. Children are usually provided for until they reach a point where they are able to take over responsibilities and enter adulthood. This is the way of things, and this is what can make Acts of Service as a love language unclear to them.

Countless times a day, educators, like family members, do acts of service for students. By their very nature and character, they do things for students without even realizing it. Most of the time they are on cruise control and the Acts of Service are a natural outcome. Students readily accept this fact and wholeheartedly receive the efforts. But receiving the efforts doesn't always equate with appreciating or understanding them! Acts of Service become commonplace for students and they often mistake them for "this is what adults are supposed to do for me." This type of thinking on their part (which is natural) creates an attitude of, "This is what we deserve." Therefore, it becomes very important that we teach students how to love others with acts of service so that we can help them change from "this is what we deserve" to "this is what we are thankful for." But how does this work?

The love languages and our working definition of love (action word) all have the same basic theme, "Loving people is intentional and not happenstance." By definition, the love language known as Acts of Service creates clearer understanding for children because it, too, shows that loving others with acts of service is intentional and not happenstance. For many children this is the first time they will ever have had to consider this concept.

The working definition of Acts of Service is "Doing something for someone that is intentional and not expected." When students first learn this definition they are faced with the notion of "not expected." This is novel to most of them. In the past when I have asked students to share with me acts of service that they have done at home, the typical responses have been: taking out the trash, emptying the dishwasher, sweeping the floor, walking the dog, etc. These examples are all good, except for one basic problem: most of the time they are examples of service that is expected of them. When I tell students that acts of service aren't chores, they usually respond with "Oh" and this begins our lesson on the topic.

We as educators can also learn from our students' misunderstandings. Doing our job doesn't necessarily mean that we are loving an Acts-of-Service child. For us to truly love a child with acts of service means that we are intentionally and unexpectedly doing something for him or her. I believe that this happens every day, but take a couple of moments and think of some examples of the last time you loved a student with acts of service. I have no doubt that you can think of something, but as we develop this working definition for all of us to use in school, we need to keep in mind that it must be intentional and not expected. This becomes very important because we want students to observe examples at home and in the school that reflect family, peers, and educational staff members who love others with acts of service. Observing others using Acts of Service starts the transformation from "we deserve" to "we are thankful." With this attitude transformation, we can start to see home and school environments where appreciation is demonstrated. Teaching about acts of service is so much more than just doing things for people; it's a way of recognizing those around us who are doing intentional and unexpected services because they love us!

Is there an opposite to Acts of Service? The answer of course is yes. All of the love languages have an opposite, and Acts of Service is no different. If the definition of Acts of Service is "doing things for people," then the opposite would be "doing things against people." For the purpose of our school setting we will call this thing "bullying."

Bullying has been addressed by public schools for years now, but the school bully issue wasn't addressed much until it got really bad. Students often lived in fear and didn't want to say anything. With the creation of new rules and reporting procedures school bullies have lost some of their power. Certainly anyone entertaining the thought of becoming a school bully has to think twice about it. The zero tolerance rules in most schools give administrators the tools that they need to enforce discipline. Students who have been trained on how to spot bullies and report them feel much more empowered. So the question remains, "Have we eradicated the school bully?" The answer is a resounding no.

School bullies still exist and they have adapted to the new rules. The line has been drawn by the schools, but the bullies have learned how to get as close to the line as possible without going over. Administrators, more than ever, are documenting any occurrences that may even remotely look like bullying. They often suspect that bullying is going on, but a single incident often isn't enough to label it as bullying. After enough evidence, administrators can then proceed ahead with disciplinary action. This can take a very long time and be quite frustrating for everyone involved, except the bully.

Students who are being bullied sometimes become confused because they aren't sure that what the bully is doing is of real consequence. Oftentimes they will wait for all the little things to add up before they say anything. By the time they do report, it's because they have had enough. Unfortunately, many times the reporting only becomes one small incident in the administrator's book of documentation. Not having documentation makes it very difficult for administrators to enforce the rules unless it is flagrant and obvious.

Each year it is the responsibility of educational staff to educate students regarding bullies. Teaching them about school rules and reporting procedures is vital. No school will ever get rid of every act of bullying, but good instruction and administration can greatly diminish it. Further, schools that teach children how to draw their personal safety lines and communicate effectively with staff members make it easier for principals to enforce the anti-bullying rules. With students and staff members trained, the school safety environment greatly increases. This training should be ongoing and conducted every year. There is a great website that has lots of useful ideas and information, it's www.stopbullying.gov, and I encourage every educator and parent to visit this website.

LESSON 4
ACTS OF SERVICE
(SCRIPTED)

OBJECTIVE:

Students will be introduced to the third love language (Acts of Service) and will be able to define what it is and how to use it. They will understand that the opposite of Acts of Service is bullying. Students will know how to apply the four steps if they think they are being bullied. Further, students will understand the school policies/procedures regarding bullying and how to report it along with other potentially dangerous events.

Write on the white board:

1. I can describe Acts of Service and how to use it.
2. I can describe bullying and can apply the four steps if I think I'm being bullied.
3. I know how to report bullying and other dangerous activities if I see them in my school.

(Have students talk with each other for thirty seconds about what they think they are going to be learning today.)

REVIEW:

Instructor will go over the previous lesson by asking volunteer students to explain:

1. What are the two goals for teaching the love languages? *(To learn your own love languages and to be able to identify the love languages of others.)*
2. What was the last love language that was taught? *(Quality Time)*
3. Review the last lesson's objectives that you wrote on the white board.
4. What is Quality Time? *(Intentional and deliberate time spent with a person to make them feel loved.)*
5. What are the four ways to make a Quality Time person feel loved? *(1. Invite them to hang out, 2. Ask them what they want to do, 3. Ask them questions about their life, 4. Be a good listener.)*

LESSON 4
ACTS OF SERVICE
(ABBREVIATED)

OBJECTIVE:

Students will be introduced to the third love language (Acts of Service) and will be able to define what it is and how to use it. They will understand that the opposite of Acts of Service is bullying. Students will know how to apply the four steps if they think they are being bullied. Further, students will understand the school policies/procedures regarding bullying and how to report it along with other potentially dangerous events.

Write on the white board:

1. I can describe Acts of Service and how to use it.
2. I can describe bullying and can apply the four steps if I think I'm being bullied.
3. I know how to report bullying and other dangerous activities if I see them in my school.

(Have students talk with each other for thirty seconds about what they think they are going to be learning today.)

REVIEW:

Instructor will go over the previous lesson by asking volunteer students to explain:

1. What are the two goals for teaching the love languages? *(To learn your own love languages and to be able to identify the love languages of others.)*
2. What was the last love language that was taught? *(Quality Time)*
3. Review the last lesson's objectives that you wrote on the white board.
4. What is Quality Time? *(Intentional and deliberate time spent with a person to make them feel loved.)*
5. What are the four ways to make a Quality Time person feel loved? *(1. Invite them to hang out, 2. Ask them what they want to do, 3. Ask them questions about their life, 4. Be a good listener.)*

6. What is the opposite of Quality Time? *(Intentionally leaving people out.)*

7. Give me an example of how you can include somebody at lunch even when they can't sit next to you. *(Politely point to a spot nearby where they can sit.)*

8. Call on a few volunteer students to quickly discuss how their assignment went and what they experienced.

9. Remind students that each time they learn a love language you want them to ask themselves: Does this love language make me feel loved or do I just like it?

ANTICIPATORY SET:

Today we are going to be learning about the third love language known as Acts of Service. *(Write "Acts of Service" on the board.)* **An act of service is doing something nice for someone that is intentional, is unexpected, and helps them out.** *(Write "intentional, unexpected, and helps them out" on the board.)*

Grade 5 or 6, continue here:	Lesson 4.0, Grade 5–6, #1

Have students write "intentional, unexpected, and helps them out" in spaces provided on the Academic Focus Page.

TEACHING/PRESENTATION:

Some people feel loved when you do nice things for them. Remember, everybody likes to have things done for them, but not everybody feels loved when this happens. Acts of Service are a way that we can make some people feel loved. When we do an act of service, we are intentionally and unexpectedly doing something nice for them that helps them out.

Now what I would like everybody to do is think about a time when someone did something nice for you that was an act of service. When you think of what they did, raise your hand, and I will write it on the board. *(Write the examples that students give on the board. Remember, they haven't learned the final two love languages (Gifts and Touch), so expect that there could be some examples in these categories. Also, some dual examples like "Making breakfast for your parents" could be considered both an act of service and a gift. If you get an answer like this, go ahead and write it down and when you are reviewing the examples given, focus on the act of service by saying, "Yes, making the breakfast would be an act of service." Further, it is highly likely that you will be given examples of things that are expected of them (e.g., chores); write these down as well. Once students have contributed a variety of answers, go through each example and clarify whether it is truly an act of service,*

6. What is the opposite of Quality Time? *(Intentionally leaving people out.)*

7. Give me an example of how you can include somebody at lunch even when they can't sit next to you. *(Politely point to a spot nearby where they can sit.)*

8. Call on a few volunteer students to quickly discuss how their assignment went and what they experienced.

9. Remind students that each time they learn a love language you want them to ask themselves: Does this love language make me feel loved or do I just like it?

ANTICIPATORY SET:

1. Introduce the love language (Acts of Service).

2. Write: "Acts of Service" on the board.

3. Write: "intentional, unexpected, and helps them out" on the board.
   • **Academic Focus Page [Lesson 4.0, Grade 5–6, #1]**

TEACHING/PRESENTATION:

1. Some people feel loved when you do Acts of Service for them.

2. Have students think of ways that people have done acts of service for them.

3. Have students volunteer answers and write them on the board.
   • **Academic Focus Page [Lesson 4.0, Grade 3–4, #1]**

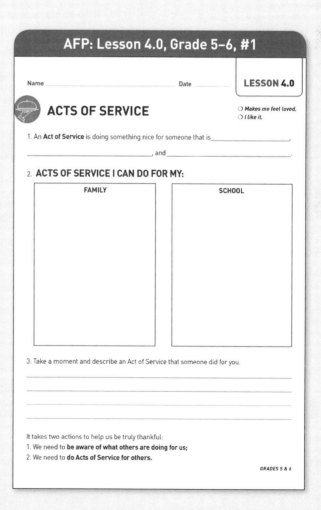

AFP: Lesson 4.0, Grade 5–6, #1

Name _____ Date _____ LESSON 4.0

ACTS OF SERVICE
○ *Makes me feel loved.*
○ *I like it.*

1. An **Act of Service** is doing something nice for someone that is_____, _____, and _____.

2. **ACTS OF SERVICE I CAN DO FOR MY:**

FAMILY	SCHOOL

3. Take a moment and describe an Act of Service that someone did for you.
_____
_____
_____

It takes two actions to help us be truly thankful:
1. We need to **be aware of what others are doing for us;**
2. We need to **do Acts of Service for others.**

GRADES 5 & 6

or something else. As you address each example given, erase the ones that aren't truly Acts of Service by explaining why they aren't. When you come to an example that is an act of service say, "Yes, this is an act of service because it is intentional, is unexpected, and helps them out." This will help students make connections between the definition and an act of service.) **These are really good examples, and thank you to everyone who took a chance and volunteered an answer. We are doing this exercise because there can be a lot of confusion when trying to understand acts of service. You would think it would be easy, but it's only easy if you ask yourself if it was intentional, was unexpected, and helped them out.**

Grade 3 or 4, continue here:	Lesson 4.0, Grade 3–4, #1

Let's see if you can figure out on your own which items are Acts of Service when you do the activity on your Academic Focus Page #1. Follow along silently as I read the directions to you. Have students circle the actions that are acts of service using our working definition. After they complete this exercise, go over each one and have students explain why this is or isn't an act of service.

Now let's talk about some things you could do for your family at home and for people here at school that would be an act of service.

Grade 1 or 2, continue here:	Lesson 4.0, Grade 1–2, Whole page

This is a teacher-directed lesson that involves whole-group instruction. On the white board, work through each category located on the Academic Focus Page. For example, "PARENTS" is the first category. Write an example for the class of an act of service they could do for their parents, e.g., "I could help my mom carry the groceries in from the car." Have students write that in the space provided. For advanced first grade students or second grade students, you can provide an example and have them write their own, or they could try to write their own without your examples.

Grade 5 or 6, continue here:	Lesson 4.0, Grade 5–6, #2

Have students write ideas for Acts of Service that they can do for their family and school in the boxes titled "FAMILY" and "SCHOOL". After they are finished ask students to contribute ideas and write them on the board (see next step below).

4. Once students have contributed a variety of answers, go through each example and clarify whether it is truly an act of service or something else. As you address each example given, erase the ones that aren't truly acts of service by explaining why they aren't. When you come to an example that is an act of service say, "Yes, this is an act of service because it is intentional, unexpected, and helps them out."

5. **Academic Focus Page Lessons:**
   • **Academic Focus Page [Lesson 4.0, Grade 1–2, Whole page]**
   • **Academic Focus Page [Lesson 4.0, Grade 5–6, #2]**

AFP: Lesson 4.0, Grade 3–4, #1

Name _____ Date _____ **LESSON 4.0**

ACTS OF SERVICE

○ Makes me feel loved.
○ I like it.

1. An **Act of Service** is doing something nice for someone that is intentional, is unexpected, and helps them out. Read the items below and circle the ones that you think are an Act of Service:

doing your chores;   taking a meal to a friend's house;   doing your brother's or sister's chores;

raking leaves at your neighbor's house without getting paid;   cleaning your bedroom;

doing the dishes at a friend's house;   watering the plants for a neighbor to earn money;

passing out papers for your teacher;   brushing your teeth;   brushing your dog's teeth;

taking care of the neighbor's pets for free;   making breakfast for your parents.

THINKING ABOUT WHAT OTHERS DO FOR US!

2. Take a moment to think about what others do for you. Hopefully this will help you to be thankful! You may be surprised at all of the Acts of Service people do for you that you weren't even aware of. Use the boxes below to write Acts of Service people do for you.

PARENTS

FRIENDS

SCHOOL STAFF

ALL OTHERS

GRADES 3 & 4

AFP: Lesson 4.0, Grade 1–2, Whole page

Name _____ Date _____ **LESSON 4.0**

ACTS OF SERVICE

○ Makes me feel loved.
○ I like it.

An **Act of Service** is doing something nice for someone that they don't expect you to do.

WHAT ARE SOME ACTS OF SERVICE YOU CAN DO FOR YOUR:

PARENTS

FRIENDS

BROTHER

SISTER

TEACHER

OTHERS

GRADES 1 & 2

AFP: Lesson 4.0, Grade 5–6, #2

Name _____ Date _____ **LESSON 4.0**

ACTS OF SERVICE

○ Makes me feel loved.
○ I like it.

1. An **Act of Service** is doing something nice for someone that is _____, _____, and _____.

2. **ACTS OF SERVICE I CAN DO FOR MY:**

FAMILY	SCHOOL

3. Take a moment and describe an Act of Service that someone did for you.

_____
_____
_____
_____

It takes two actions to help us be truly thankful:
1. We need to **be aware of what others are doing for us;**
2. We need to **do Acts of Service for others.**

GRADES 5 & 6

(On the board, make two columns and write the words FAMILY and SCHOOL. Under each column heading, write the ideas that the students contribute. You will use this list of ideas later for the assignment.) [DO NOT ERASE THESE EXAMPLES!] **These are great examples, and we will come back to them at the end of the lesson.**

Sometimes organizations can do Acts of Service for individuals or groups of people. These organizations are made up of different people who get together because they care and want to help others. Some examples of these would be First Tee, Kiwanis Club, Habitat for Humanity, YMCA, YWCA, Meals on Wheels, Ronald McDonald House, and animal shelters. Organizations usually have a goal of helping certain groups of people. For example, First Tee is a youth organization that promotes life skills and leadership through the game of golf. Ronald McDonald House helps families who need a place to stay when their children are hospitalized. And animal shelters help animals that need a loving home. Many individuals find it easier to help large groups of people when they are part of a team and volunteer their time to help with a cause. Kids can volunteer as well. If you would be interested in volunteering, you could ask your parents, church leaders, or teachers for ideas. All of the organizations I just talked about have websites, and with permission you can go online and read more about them. Volunteering your time is a great way to perform an act of service in a big way!

When people perform Acts of Service, it makes a huge difference in many lives. Probably the biggest difference will be in your own life. When you try to love someone with an act of service, it has a way of making you feel good about yourself, whether it's the other person's love language or not. Doing Acts of Service reminds us that we don't always have to have things done for us but that we are willing to give to others by doing things for them. Another great thing about doing Acts of Service is it makes us thankful for those who do things for us. After you have put in some of your own time doing an act of service, you realize that it's not always that easy, and it makes you appreciate what others do for you. It's like your eyes have been opened to see all the things that people do for you. It just makes you want to say, "Thank you." Did you know if you say "Thank you" to someone, you are really saying, "I appreciate what you are doing for me." You recognize their act of service and acknowledge it with your words. And people who do Acts of Service are encouraged when they hear those words!

Unfortunately, some kids *aren't* in the habit of thinking about the needs of other people, and this can make them appear selfish. Think about it for a moment. If someone only lets people do things for them and never does anything for anyone else, doesn't that look selfish? I think some kids don't even notice what other people are doing for them. Nobody wants to look selfish or ungrateful, but some kids do look like this. If you are someone who has never thought about acts of service done for you, then you should take a moment and think about it. Thinking about this will help to

6. Make two columns on the board labeled "family" and "school."

7. Have students volunteer examples of what they can do for others at home and at school. Write these examples under the appropriate heading.

8. Discuss various service organizations and their benefits to individuals and large groups of people such as First Tee and Ronald McDonald House. Point out that kids can volunteer too!

9. Doing Acts of Service reminds us that we don't always have to have things done for us but that we are willing to give to others by doing things for them.

10. Doing Acts of Service makes us thankful for what others do for us.

11. When you say "Thank you" to someone, you are really saying, "I appreciate what you are doing for me."

12. Students who are unaware of what others do for them appear selfish and ungrateful.

make you thankful for others and what they do for you. In order for our homes, school, or anywhere else to be a great place, we need to be the kind of people who notice what others are doing for us. Remember, it takes two things to show that we are truly thankful: (1) We need to be aware of what others are doing for us, and (2) We actually need to be doing acts of service for others. In the process of doing these two things, some people will not only feel like you care, they may even feel loved! *(Write on board: 1. Be aware of what others are doing for you. 2. Do Acts of Service for others.)*

Grade 3 or 4, continue here: Lesson 4.0, Grade 3–4, #2

"Look at the second activity on your Academic Focus Page. Read the directions silently to yourself as I read them aloud." Have students write, in each of the spaces provided, Acts of Service that they have observed others doing for them. Remind them of the definition (intentional, unexpected, helps them out) as they write their examples. When they finish, have volunteers share with the class ideas that they came up with. The "ALL OTHERS" category may be the most interesting since this requires the students to think of other people not listed that have done acts of service for them. Be on the lookout for examples that don't fit the definition. Help students understand why it doesn't fit the definition.

Grade 5 or 6, continue here: Lesson 4.0, Grade 5–6, #3

"Look at the third activity on your Academic Focus Page. Read the directions silently to yourself as I read them aloud." Have students take a moment to describe an act of service that someone did for them. When they finish, have volunteers share with the class ideas that they came up with. Be on the lookout for examples that don't fit the definition. Help students understand why it doesn't fit the definition.

[TRANSITION TO OPPOSITE]

ANTICIPATORY SET:

Now we need to talk about a negative behavior, or opposite of Acts of Service. If our definition of Acts of Service is to do something for others, then the opposite of this would be to do something to others. If when we do Acts of Service we are trying to help a person, then the opposite of this would be to hurt a person. For the purpose of this lesson, we will call this negative behavior "bullying."

13. Students should take a moment and think about all of the things people do for them.

14. It takes two things to show that we are truly thankful. *(Write on board: 1. Be aware of what others are doing for you. 2. Do acts of service for others.)*
   • **Academic Focus Page [Lesson 4.0, Grade 3–4, #2]**
   • **Academic Focus Page [Lesson 4.0, Grade 5–6, #3]**

AFP: Lesson 4.0, Grade 3–4, #2

Name _____ Date _____   **LESSON 4.0**

ACTS OF SERVICE

○ *Makes me feel loved.*
○ *I like it.*

1. An **Act of Service** is doing something nice for someone that is intentional, is unexpected, and helps them out. Read the items below and circle the ones that you think are an Act of Service:

doing your chores;   taking a meal to a friend's house;   doing your brother's or sister's chores;

raking leaves at your neighbor's house without getting paid;   cleaning your bedroom;

doing the dishes at a friend's house;   watering the plants for a neighbor to earn money;

passing out papers for your teacher;   brushing your teeth;   brushing your dog's teeth;

taking care of the neighbor's pets for free;   making breakfast for your parents.

THINKING ABOUT WHAT OTHERS DO FOR US!

2. Take a moment to think about what others do for you. Hopefully this will help you to be thankful! You may be surprised at all of the Acts of Service people do for you that you weren't even aware of. Use the boxes below to write Acts of Service people do for you.

PARENTS	
SCHOOL STAFF	
FRIENDS	
ALL OTHERS	

GRADES 3 & 4

AFP: Lesson 4.0, Grade 5–6, #3

Name _____ Date _____   **LESSON 4.0**

ACTS OF SERVICE

○ *Makes me feel loved.*
○ *I like it.*

1. An **Act of Service** is doing something nice for someone that is_____, _____, and _____.

2. **ACTS OF SERVICE I CAN DO FOR MY:**

FAMILY	SCHOOL

3. Take a moment and describe an Act of Service that someone did for you.

_____

_____

_____

It takes two actions to help us be truly thankful:
1. We need to **be aware of what others are doing for us;**
2. We need to **do Acts of Service for others.**

GRADES 5 & 6

[TRANSITION TO OPPOSITE]

ANTICIPATORY SET:

1. Opposite of Acts of Service: helping people vs. hurting people.

2. We call this negative behavior "bullying" (write it on board).

3. Write definition of bully on the board (one habitually cruel to others who are weaker).

TEACHING/PRESENTATION:

Many of you have heard the word "bullying" before. Bullying sounds like bowling but bullying actually has a "y" in it to give it a long (e) sound. *(Write "Bullying" on the board.)* We get the word "bullying" from the word "bully." In the dictionary I found this definition of what a bully is: one habitually cruel to others who are weaker. *(Write this definition on the board.)* What this means is that a bully is someone who is cruel or mean to others on a regular basis.

When someone acts like a bully or is bullying someone, they are trying to be cruel to that person. Who is the bully being cruel to? Read the definition and raise your hand when you have the answer. What is the answer? *(Others who are weaker.)* Right, others who are weaker. And how often does a bully do the bullying? *(Habitually; this means on a regular basis.)* So a bully picks on weaker people all of the time. But notice that the definition of a bully doesn't include how they are being cruel. Why do you think that is? *(Because there are too many behaviors to define as cruel.)* A definition can't begin to list all the ways that a bully could be cruel. There are too many possibilities. It could be anything from hitting someone, to looking at them weird. So it's really up to the person being bullied to determine if they are being bullied or not. And notice that the definition doesn't say whether the bully is a boy or girl, man or woman. Why is this? *(Because it can be any of those people.)* So we have figured out that a bully can be anyone who does something cruel on a regular basis. But sometimes students get confused and can't figure out if someone is being a bully. Sometimes they think that the student might just be being annoying or messing around. And sometimes a student who bothers someone else says that they were just joking or messing around or kidding. But how can you tell if that's true or not? *(Rhetorical)* I'm going to teach you a strategy that can help you figure that out, and then I'm going to teach you what to do about it. Okay, here we go:

1. When somebody does something to you that you don't like but you're not sure if they are doing it to be mean, tell them to "Stop." This is called drawing your personal safety line. *(I usually draw a pretend line in front of me with both hands and say, "I'm telling them that this is my line and not to go any farther.")* When you tell someone to stop, you need to say it in a serious voice. *(Demonstrate a serious voice.)*

2. Walk or move away from the person who was bothering you.

3. If the person who was bothering you still follows you, tell them to leave you alone in a serious voice.

4. If they continue to follow you or bother you, tell _____ *(insert specific school reporting procedure here).*

TEACHING/PRESENTATION:

1. Ask the class: Who is the bully being cruel too? *(someone weaker)*

2. Ask the class: How often is a bully cruel? *(on a regular basis)*

3. Ask the class: Why doesn't the definition of a bully include how they are being cruel? *(There are too many possibilities.)*

4. Say: The definition doesn't say whether a bully is a boy or girl, man or woman. Why is this? *(It could be anyone.)*

5. Say: We have determined that a bully can be anyone who is cruel to others on a regular basis.

6. Say: Sometimes figuring out if you are being bullied can be confusing.

7. Go over the four steps:
   1. Draw your personal safety line by saying "Stop" in a serious voice.
   2. Walk or move away from the person who is bothering you.
   3. If the person who was bothering you still follows you, tell them to leave you alone in a serious voice.
   4. If they continue to follow you or bother you, tell _____ *(insert school reporting procedures).*

Grades 1–6, continue here: | Lesson 4.1, Grades 1–6, A–D

"I'm going to go over the four steps again and this time I want you to fill out the spaces on your Academic Support Page A–D." After you read each step have them fill in the blank. If you are teaching first or second grade, write the answers in a place where they can see them and copy them onto the page. After students are finished writing these four steps have them role-play with a partner. One student is the bully and the other student is the victim. You can demonstrate how this would look with students by role-playing with a student in front of the class. Have partners switch roles so each gets a turn to practice the four steps.

It's important to follow these four basic steps because if you don't draw your personal safety line and tell someone to stop, they may not know that you were serious. Plus, when you tell them to stop and they continue to bother you, then you know they are being mean to you on a regular basis. And from what we learned from our definition, a bully is someone who is being mean to weaker people on a regular basis. This would be true if the bully did something to you tomorrow, or in two days, or next week, or even in a month, after you told him or her to stop.

Everyone in our school has a right to learn and be safe. Our school considers bullying a very serious offense. We have school rules to deal with bullies. *(Insert school rules/policy here.)* Sometimes kids don't tell us about a bully because they are too scared. They think that if they tell someone, the bully might do something even worse. So the bully keeps being mean to the weaker kids and hurting their lives.

If someone is being cruel or mean to you, we want to know. Bring a friend with you, or have your parents call us, because we want to know. If you are a student who sees someone being bullied, we want you to report it. *(Insert school reporting procedure here.)* Remember how Acts of Service is doing something nice for someone else by helping them out? By telling someone about a bully, you could be doing an act of service for a person who you don't even know! And by the way, this goes for anything dangerous that you happen to see at our school. We want you to do an act of service for all of our students by reporting it and keeping them safe. *(In the past I have used this opportunity to tie in the situation of seeing a weapon (real/toy) brought to school and what the reporting procedures are. I call this "an act of service to your school.")* **Are there any questions?**

8. **Academic Focus Page:**
   [Lesson 4.1, Grade 1–6, A–D]

9. Say: "It's important to follow these four basic steps because some people don't know that what they are doing is bothering you."

10. Say: "Everyone in our school has a right to learn and be safe. Our school takes bullying very seriously."

11. Say: "We have school rules to deal with bullies." *(Insert school policy.)*

12. Say: "Students feel too scared to report what is happening to them. But we want to know if this is happening to you. You can always:
    • Bring a friend with you to report what happened if that makes you feel more comfortable.
    • Tell your parent(s) and have them contact us. "

13. Say: "If you are a student who sees someone else being bullied, we want to know about that." *(Insert school reporting procedure.)*

14. Say: "Report any dangerous activity that you see at school. This is your act of service to the entire school."

15. Say: "Any questions?"

AFP: Lesson 4.1, Grade 1–2, A–D

Name _____ Date _____

LESSON 4.1
HOME CONNECTION SECTION

ACTS OF SERVICE

1. The definition of **Acts of Service** is to do something kind for others by helping them out. The opposite would be doing something cruel to others or hurting them in some way. This could be verbally, emotionally, or physically. We call this negativve behavior "bullying."

WHAT WOULD YOU DO TO STOP A BULLY?

A. I would tell them to _____ in a serious voice.

B. I would _____ or _____ away from the person.

C. If the person still follows me I would tell them to _____ in a serious voice.

D. If they continue to follow or bother me I would tell _____ .

AFP: Lesson 4.1, Grade 3–4, A–D

Name _____ Date _____

LESSON 4.1
HOME CONNECTION SECTION

ACTS OF SERVICE

1. The definition of **Acts of Service** is to do something kind for others by helping them out. The opposite would be doing something cruel to others or hurting them in some way. This could be verbally, emotionally, or physically. We call this negative behavior "bullying."

WHAT WOULD YOU DO TO STOP A BULLY?

A. I would tell them to _____ in a serious voice.

B. I would _____ or _____ away from the person.

C. If the person still follows me I would tell them to _____ in a serious voice.

D. If they continue to follow or bother me I would tell _____ .

AFP: Lesson 4.1, Grade 5–6, A–D

Name _____ Date _____

LESSON 4.1
HOME CONNECTION SECTION

ACTS OF SERVICE

1. The definition of **Acts of Service** is to do something kind for others by helping them out. The opposite would be doing something cruel to others or hurting them in some way. This could be verbally, emotionally, or physically. We call this negative behavior "bullying."

WHAT WOULD YOU DO TO STOP A BULLY?

A. I would tell them to _____ in a serious voice.

B. I would _____ or _____ away from the person.

C. If the person still follows me I would tell them to _____ in a serious voice.

D. If they continue to follow or bother me I would tell _____ .

OUR SCHOOL TAKES SAFETY SERIOUSLY!
HERE IS A TEST TO SEE IF YOU KNOW SOME UNUSUAL FACTS ABOUT BULLYING.

TRUE or FALSE   If I see a bully hurting someone else, I should ignore it because it isn't really hurting me.

TRUE or FALSE   Sending a cruel text message could be a form of bullying.

TRUE or FALSE   If someone bullies a person in the neighborhood, it's not really the school's concern.

TRUE or FALSE   Bullies are always physically bigger than the person they are bullying.

ALWAYS REPORT BULLYING OR ANY DANGEROUS ACTIVITY to an adult. At school, this can be your teacher or anyone else who works at the school. At home, this can be any adult who is a family member, relative, or guardian.

STOP BULLIES! ALWAYS TELL SOMEONE!

GRADES 5 & 6

Grades 1–6, continue here: Lesson 4.1, Grades 1–6, True/False Questions

"Now I'm going to have you take a quick true/false test to see if you know some unusual facts about bullying." Read the four test questions to the students and have them circle the answer they think is correct. Go over each answer and give the following explanations *(encourage whole group discussion)*:

- If I see a bully hurting someone else . . . (False) Not reporting bullying hurts everyone. It creates a school environment that feels unsafe and people can't concentrate on learning and having fun. Not reporting a bully gives the bully a chance to make you or one of your friends the next target. We have a responsibility to be a good neighbor to someone else and protect them by reporting.

- Sending a cruel text message . . . (True) Bullying can happen in many forms including something called "cyber bullying." Cyber bullying refers to any harassment that occurs via the Internet, cellphones, or other devices.

- If someone bullies a person in the neighborhood . . . (False) The school cares about all of its students on and off the school grounds. Bullying that happens off school grounds can directly influence how a student behaves at school. If the person bullying is a student from a different school it's still important to report it.

- Bullies are always physically bigger . . . (False) A bully can come in any size. Small people can still text or threaten someone. It's not based on size or if it's a boy or girl. A bully can be anyone who is acting cruelly to another person.

Grade 5 or 6, continue here: Lesson 4.2, Grade 5–6, Whole Page

"Look at your Student Support Page 4.2. Read the directions silently to yourself as I read them aloud." This is a compare/contrast lesson. Have students do this assignment with a friend. Tell them to include at least one cyber bullying example. Have the teams share their answers with the rest of the class.

CLOSURE:

Today we learned about Acts of Service. Acts of Service can play a significant role in making people feel good about themselves, but most importantly it makes some people feel loved. An act of service is a nice thing that you do for someone that is intentional, is unexpected, and helps them out. Examples could include getting someone a glass of water, sweeping the driveway, or writing down what the homework assignment is for a classmate. Students who see things that need to be done and do them without being asked are practicing Acts of Service. These students are usually

16. **Academic Focus Pages:**
- Academic Focus Page [Lesson 4.1, Grade 1–6, True/False Questions]
- Academic Focus Page [Lesson 4.2, Grade 5–6, Whole Page]

AFP: Lesson 4.1, Grade 1–2, True/False Qs

Name _____ Date _____

LESSON 4.1
HOME CONNECTION SECTION

ACTS OF SERVICE

1. The definition of **Acts of Service** is to do something kind for others by helping them out. The opposite would be doing something cruel to others or hurting them in some way. This could be verbally, emotionally, or physically. We call this negativve behavior "bullying."

WHAT WOULD YOU DO TO STOP A BULLY?

A. I would tell them to _____ in a serious voice.

B. I would _____ or _____ away from the person.

C. If the person still follows me I would tell them to _____ in a serious voice.

D. If they continue to follow or bother me I would tell _____.

OUR SCHOOL TAKES SAFETY SERIOUSLY!

HERE IS A TEST TO SEE IF YOU KNOW SOME UNUSUAL FACTS ABOUT BULLYING.

TRUE or FALSE   If I see a bully hurting someone else, I should ignore it because it isn't really hurting me.

TRUE or FALSE   Sending a cruel text message could be a form of bullying.

TRUE or FALSE   If someone bullies a person in the neighborhood, it's not really the school's concern.

TRUE or FALSE   Bullies are always physically bigger than the person they are bullying.

ALWAYS REPORT BULLYING OR ANY DANGEROUS ACTIVITY to an adult. At school, this can be your teacher or anyone else who works at the school. At home, this can be any adult who is a family member, relative, or guardian.

STOP BULLIES! ALWAYS TELL SOMEONE!

GRADES 1–6

AFP: Lesson 4.2, Grade 5–6, Whole Page

Name _____ Date _____

LESSON 4.2
HOME CONNECTION SECTION

ACTS OF SERVICE

1. The definition of **Acts of Service** is to do something kind for others by helping them out. The opposite would be to do something cruel to others or hurt them in some way. This could be verbally, emotionally, or physically. We call this negative behavior "bullying." (In the following shapes compare and contrast the difference between Acts of Service and Bullying. Write specific examples to show that you know the difference between each of them. One of the examples needs to involve cyber bullying.)

ACTS OF SERVICE	BULLYING BEHAVIOR
Example: Helping someone get up when they fall down.	*Example: Tripping someone.*

(four empty boxes under each column)

ALWAYS REPORT BULLYING OR ANY DANGEROUS ACTIVITY to an adult. At school, this can be your teacher or anyone else that works at the school. At home, this can be any adult that is a family member, relative, or guardian.

STOP BULLIES! ALWAYS TELL SOMEONE!

GRADES 5 & 6

CLOSURE:

Today we learned about Acts of Service. Acts of Service can play a significant role in making people feel good about themselves, but most importantly it makes some people feel loved. An act of service is a nice thing that you do for someone that is intentional, is unexpected, and helps them out. Examples could include getting someone a glass of water, sweeping the driveway, or writing down what the homework assignment is for a classmate. Students who see things that need to be done and do them without being asked are practicing Acts of Service. These students are usually thankful for the things that are done for them. **Students who don't take the time to see what is done for them can often appear ungrateful or selfish. These students should take a moment and figure out what acts of service people are doing for them. When we perform acts of service, it makes us thankful, and this in turn makes our home, school, and anywhere else a nice place to be.**

We also learned about bullies. A bully can be anyone who is trying to be cruel to a weaker person on a regular basis. We learned that there are four steps to use if you are unsure that you are being bullied: 1. Draw your personal safety line and tell them to "Stop" in a serious voice. 2. Walk or move away from them. 3. If the person still follows you, tell them to leave you alone. 4. If they continue to follow or bother you, tell _____ *(insert reporting procedure here).*

You also learned that our school takes bullying very seriously. We want all of our students to be safe. Some students may be too afraid to tell someone. Those students should take a friend with them to report, or they should tell their parents. If anyone observes another person being bullied, we want you to report it. If you see any type of dangerous behavior, we want you to report that as well. When a student reports bullies or dangerous situations, they are doing an act of service for the whole school.

Ask yourself, "When people do things for me, does it make me feel loved or do I just really like it?" Please fill in a circle by one of the items at the top right-hand side of your Academic Focus Page. The items say, "Makes me feel loved," or "I like it."

Now, let's talk about the assignment.

INDEPENDENT PRACTICE/ASSIGNMENT:

Each student will be doing an act of service at home and school.

1. Tell the students that you want them to practice acts of service at home and school.
2. The act of service at home can be for any family member.
3. The act of service at school can be for anyone in the school.
4. Remind students that it's not necessary to explain to people that this is for an assignment.
5. Go over the list of examples that you wrote on the board to give students ideas about what they can do for their act of service. Tell them that they are not limited to this list or to doing only one thing at home or school.
6. Tell students when you will return to teach the next lesson. Remind them that you will be asking various students about their experience the next time you teach the love languages.
7. Review the objectives written on the white board. Make sure students are clear about the three objectives with special emphasis on reporting.

thankful for the things that are done for them. Students who don't take the time to see what is done for them can often appear ungrateful or selfish. These students should take a moment and figure out what acts of service people are doing for them. When we perform acts of service it makes us thankful, and this in turn makes our home, school, and anywhere else a nice place to be.

We also learned about bullies. A bully can be anyone who is trying to be cruel to a weaker person on a regular basis. We learned that there are four steps to use if you are unsure that you are being bullied: 1. Draw your personal safety line and tell them to "Stop" in a serious voice. 2. Walk or move away from them. 3. If the person still follows you, tell them to leave you alone. 4. If they continue to follow or bother you, tell _____ (insert reporting procedure here).

You also learned that our school takes bullying very serious. We want all of our students to be safe. Some students may be too afraid to tell someone. Those students should take a friend with them to report, or tell their parents. If anyone observes another person being bullied, we want you to report it. If you see any type of dangerous behavior we want you to report that as well. When a student reports bullies or dangerous situations, they are doing an act of service for the whole school.

Ask yourself, "When people do things for me, does it make me feel loved or do I just really like it?" Please fill in a circle by one of the items at the top right-hand side of your Academic Focus Page. The items say, "Makes me feel loved," or "I like it."

Now let's look at the assignment:

INDEPENDENT PRACTICE/ASSIGNMENT:

Each student will be doing an act of service at home and school.

1. Tell the students that you want them to practice acts of service at home and school.
2. The act of service at home can be for any family member.
3. The act of service at school can be for anyone in the school.
4. Remind students that it's not necessary to explain to people that this is for an assignment.
5. Go over the list of examples that you wrote on the board to give students ideas about what they can do for their act of service. Tell them that they are not limited to this list or to doing only one thing at home or school.
6. Tell students when you will return to teach the next lesson. Remind them that you will be asking various students about their experience the next time you teach the love languages.
7. Review the objectives written on the white board. Make sure students are clear about the three objectives with special emphasis on reporting.

FINAL THOUGHTS

Teaching about the love language Acts of Service can create a markedly better environment for students and staff members. Although this is true for all of the love languages, Acts of Service tends to be slightly different in that it creates a community of learners who are thankful. Something special happens when people start looking out for each other and finding ways to help.

I find that most students really want to help people. Oftentimes they don't know how. When teaching this lesson, have a lot of different examples of acts of service at your disposal, just in case the students can't generate very many. Some students may be too young to really come up with a lot of things that they can do. [Consult with the list of examples in the back of this book.]

Regarding the bullying section, you may want to bring your administrator on board. Administrators have access to school policies and reporting procedures. Even if you know policies/procedures by heart, remember that administrators work with them daily. They can bring valuable insight and wisdom to this section of the lesson. They may also want to meet with other staff members to tell them about what is being taught in the classroom. Staff members and supervisors may be surprised at the sudden increase in the amount of events that are being reported. Raising awareness with students will bring issues out into the open. A few students will misunderstand and think that some students are being bullies when they really aren't. This usually happens to a minimal extent and will fade with time and guidance. The majority of students will understand what was taught and only report when it's legitimate.

There's a section of the bullying lesson that describes a bully as being anyone—child or adult, male or female. This is purposeful because it builds a foundation that will be continued in the lesson on touch. As most educators know, sometimes when children are abused there can be a bully involved, especially if they are a teenager/adult. You want your students to have the mindset that if someone is doing something that crosses their personal safety line, it's not okay. A bully doesn't necessarily have to be in attendance at school.

FROM THE CLASSROOM

My school tends to be big on Acts of Service. This is because the community we live in makes it a top priority to be involved. There have been times during the school day when there can be up to 100 parent volunteers in the school. Their children have had excellent role models.

One organization that we have in our community is Kiwanis Club. It has an offshoot for grade school children called K-Kids. It's an excellent organization that does a variety of services that directly help people in need. If you don't have a club in your area, I would strongly encourage you to start one. The nice thing about K-Kids is that it offers children a chance to serve when they might not be able to otherwise. Organizations like K-Kids are run by adult volunteers from outside the school and are usually assisted by one or two volunteer staff members. The students do the majority of the work, which includes electing officers and planning agendas. It's a great way for students to practice Acts of Service on a large scale.

When I think of acts of service, one girl especially stands out to me. This girl won the Principal Award for best all-around student. What makes this girl so amazing is how often she would look for ways to assist other students. Many of us at the award assembly knew whom the principal was describing. The description of this girl was so profound and so true, it couldn't possibly be anyone else. What stands out so much to me about this girl is her ability to do acts of service on a regular basis. She helped new students find their way, she would put her arm around students when they were sad, and she seemed to always have a smile on her face, followed with a kind word. A student who demonstrates some of these qualities occasionally is considered remarkable, but one who does it on a regular basis is way over the top. What even impressed me more about this student is that she served others, knowing that her mom had been diagnosed with cancer, her little brother struggled with autism, and her arm broke while playing soccer. Most of us would be crushed, but this girl obviously understands what it means to love people with Acts of Service. There has to be a lesson in here for all of us.

CHAPTER 6
Gifts

INTRODUCTION

People who feel loved by receiving gifts usually don't like to talk about it. I have often been told by them that they feel selfish for having this as their love language. While teaching this lesson, keep in mind that some of your students may be feeling uneasy.

Virtually everyone has a profound story that relates to the love language known as Gifts. Whether a person is young or old, it's very likely that a significant gift experience has occurred in their life. Gifts have a tremendous impact because they are more than material items. When gifts are given, they become positive or negative symbols. On the positive side, they can represent appreciation, value, sacrifice, love, devotion, apologies, or celebration. On the negative side they can represent guilt, bribery, failure, thoughtlessness, fear, or cruelty. If the person giving the gifts is valued by the receiver, then the gifts are always received as an extension of the giver. For the purpose of this chapter the focus will be narrowed to giving gifts to people who are known, loved, and cared about. Giving gifts to acquaintances can look very different, although many of the concepts still hold true.

Because gifts represent more than material items, it is very important that each person learns to perfect the art of gift-giving. It's vital that it isn't written off as something only others can do. It is necessary to grasp the deeper meanings involved and find gifts that match the recipient. Giving good gifts takes a great deal of thoughtfulness. Many a person has been hurt by others who weren't willing to learn the art of giving. It may be that many have failed at gift-giving due to the confusion as to what makes a good gift.

Perhaps much of this confusion about gifts lies within our society where marketing runs rampant. Marketers have the responsibility to create felt needs for people so that they can sell products. One basic marketing message implies that buying items will make people feel loved (just watch the television for jewelry commercials!). Marketers realize that most purchases are made with some sort of emotional connection between the consumer and the seller. They spend billions of dollars trying to get people connected emotionally with their name. If consumers go to make a purchase and are unsure about what to buy, marketers are hoping that people will rely on marketing to help guide them. Unfortunately the message that says, "Everybody will feel loved when you buy a certain item," leaves many buyers feeling like they've failed after purchasing and giving the gift. Making decisions about getting gifts should be done based on what is known about a person, not on what advertisements say. Like all love languages, the more specific and personal, the more loved the recipient feels.

What most people with the love language of Gifts want others to know is that they value being known. They feel loved because someone took the time and effort to get them something. Excellent gift-giving is only accomplished by getting to know someone well. And, getting to know someone requires a detective-like attitude that includes careful listening and a keen eye.

On the other hand, no one should be paralyzed by fear and fail to give a gift because they are uncertain that the recipient will like it or that it doesn't cost enough. Not knowing exactly what a person wants is not an excuse. "Gift" people love spur-of-the-moment purchases that are random and unexpected. They love to be surprised by an item that suddenly shows up. A gift person will appreciate the fact that an effort was made to get them something. When it is discovered that someone's love language is gifts, they should purposefully receive more gifts than the average person.

If your experience is similar to mine, you will find that very few students have gifts as their primary love language. When I first started teaching the love languages, I was told by several colleagues that most of the children in my school would choose Gifts as their primary love language. This couldn't have been further from the truth! After conducting a school-wide survey, we discovered that the majority of children didn't feel loved by receiving gifts. Yes, they really liked to get them but when it came down to it, the gift didn't make them feel loved. This serves as a profound reminder that children are able to figure out what they "like" as opposed to what makes them feel "loved." Now let's discover who feels loved by getting gifts and encourage them to be proud of their love language.

LESSON 5
GIFTS
(SCRIPTED)

OBJECTIVE:

Students will be able to understand and describe the love language known as "Gifts." Further, they will understand the deeper meaning of a gift and why it makes some people feel loved. They will be able to describe what bribery is and learn how to use the four basic steps when encountering it.

Write on the white board:

1. I can explain to people why gifts make some people feel loved.
2. I can describe bribery.
3. I know the four steps if someone tries to bribe me.

(Have students talk with each other for thirty seconds about what they think they are going to be learning today.)

REVIEW:

Instructor will ask volunteer students to explain:

1. What are the two goals for teaching the love languages? *(To learn your own love languages and to be able to identify the love languages of others.)*
2. What was the last love language that was taught? *(Acts of Service)*
3. Review the last lesson's objectives that you wrote on the white board.
4. What are acts of service? *(An act of service is doing something nice for someone that is intentional, is unexpected, and helps them out.)*
5. What are some examples of Acts of Service? *(answers vary)*
6. What is considered a negative behavior that is opposite of Acts of Service? *(Bullying)*
7. What do you do if you see or experience this negative behavior? *(Answers should align with school policy.)*

LESSON 5
GIFTS
(ABBREVIATED)

OBJECTIVE:

Students will be able to understand and describe the love language known as "Gifts." Further, they will understand the deeper meaning of a gift and why it makes some people feel loved. They will be able to describe what bribery is and learn how to use the four basic steps when encountering it.

Write on the white board:

1. I can explain to people why gifts make some people feel loved.
2. I can describe bribery.
3. I know the four steps if someone tries to bribe me.

(Have students talk with each other for thirty seconds about what they think they are going to be learning today.)

REVIEW:

Instructor will ask volunteer students to explain:

1. What are the two goals for teaching the love languages? *(To learn your own love languages and to be able to identify the love languages of others.)*
2. What was the last love language that was taught? *(Acts of Service)*
3. Review the last lesson's objectives you wrote on the white board.
4. What are acts of service? *(An act of service is doing something nice for someone that is intentional, is unexpected, and helps them out.)*
5. What are some examples of Acts of Service? *(answers vary)*
6. What is considered a negative behavior that is opposite of Acts of Service? *(Bullying)*
7. What do you do if you see or experience this negative behavior? *(Answers should align with school policy.)*

8. Call on a few volunteer students to quickly discuss how their assignment went and what they experienced.

9. Remind students that each time they learn a love language you want them to ask themselves: Does this love language make me feel loved or do I just like it?

ANTICIPATORY SET:

Today we will be learning about the love language called Gifts. *(Write "Gifts" on the board.)* **How many of you really like to receive gifts?** *(Rhetorical)* **Like all of the love languages, some people, not all, feel really loved when they get gifts. Gifts are more than just material items or things. Gifts represent the one who is giving it. They become a symbol of appreciation, value, sacrifice, love, devotion, apologies, celebration, etc. For some of you in here, this may be your love language. Let's find out.**

Grade 1 or 2, continue here:	Lesson 5.0, Grade 1–2, Whole Page

Have students fill in the shapes with gifts that they would really like to receive. Have them write a sentence or two explaining why they picked one of their gifts. Have students turn to a neighbor and tell them what their favorite gift is and why. Call on individuals to share with the class what they picked and why. This activity really gets students interested in the lesson. Students like it when the instructor talks about what four gifts they would like to receive.

Grade 3 or 4, continue here:	Lesson 5.0, Grade 3–4, #1

"Look at lesson 5.0, and read the directions silently while I read them aloud." Have students describe in a few sentences what gift they would pick if they could have any gift in the world, then have them draw a picture of it. Have students turn to a neighbor and tell them about what they picked and why. Call on individuals to show their pictures and describe the gift. This activity really gets students interested in the lesson. Students like it when the instructor talks about what they would pick.

8. Call on a few volunteer students to quickly discuss how their assignment went and what they experienced.

9. Remind students that each time they learn a love language you want them to ask themselves: Does this love language make me feel loved, or do I just like it?

ANTICIPATORY SET:

1. Introduce the love language of Gifts.

2. Write "Gifts" on the board.
   • More than a material item.
   • Represent the giver.
   • Gifts become a symbol.

3. **Academic Focus Pages**
   • **Academic Focus Page [Lesson 5.0, Grade 1–2, Whole Page]**
   • **Academic Focus Page [Lesson 5.0, Grade 3–4, #1]**
   • **Academic Focus Page [Lesson 5.0, Grade 5–6, #1]**

AFP: Lesson 5.0, Grade 1–2, Whole Page

Name _____ Date _____ **LESSON 5.0**

🎁 **GIFTS** ○ *Makes me feel loved.*
○ *I like it.*

1.

(diagram) GIFTS I REALLY WANT!

2. Why did you pick these gifts? Pick one gift and tell us why you picked it.

_____

_____

//

BRIBERY
HOME CONNECTION SECTION

Bribery is a negative behavior. It means that someone is trying to give a gift to get you to do something or get something from you. You should always ask your parents' permission before receiving a gift. If someone wants to give you a gift and you don't have permission then follow these three simple steps:

A. Politely refuse the gift by saying, "No, thank you." Tell them that your parents don't allow you to take gifts or money without their permission.

B. Tell your parents that someone offered you a gift.

C. If someone in a car tries to offer you a gift to go with them, scream and run away. Try to find help. Do not spend any time talking to them and don't get close to their car.

GRADES 1 & 2

AFP: Lesson 5.0, Grade 3–4, #1

Name _____ Date _____ **LESSON 5.0**

🎁 **GIFTS** ○ *Makes me feel loved.*
○ *I like it.*

1. If you could have ANY gift in the world, what would it be and why?

_____

_____

DRAW A PICTURE OF YOUR GIFT AND LABEL IT

//

BRIBERY
HOME CONNECTION SECTION

Bribery is a negative behavior. It means that someone is trying to give a gift to get you to do something or get something from you. You should always ask your parents' permission before receiving a gift. If someone wants to give you a gift and you don't have permission then follow these three simple steps:

A. Politely refuse the gift by saying, "No, thank you." Tell them that your parents don't allow you to take gifts or money without their permission.

B. Tell your parents that someone offered you a gift.

C. If someone in a car tries to offer you a gift to go with them, scream and run away. Try to find help. Do not spend any time talking to them and don't get close to their car.

GRADES 3 & 4

Grade 5 or 6, continue here: Lesson 5.0, Grade 5–6, #1

"Look at lesson 5.0, and read the directions silently while I read them aloud."
Have students describe the best gift they ever received and why they received it. If
their answer is, "I asked for it," have them go deeper and explain to you why they
asked for it. What did they think it would do for them, make them feel, etc.? Have
students turn to a neighbor and tell them what the gift was and why they received
it. Call on individual students to share their answers. This activity really gets
students interested in the lesson. Students like it when the instructor talks about
what they received.

TEACHING/PRESENTATION:

**Let's start out by talking about some special occasions when people give and receive
gifts. What are some of these occasions?** *(Birthdays, religious holidays, wedding showers,
baby showers, Mother's Day, Father's Day, etc.)* **I want you to think for a moment. Why do
we give gifts on these days?** *(To show people that we love them, care, appreciate, celebrate,
etc.)* **Would you say that it's important to give gifts on these days?** *(Rhetorical)* **Why?**
(Yes, it's cultural and it would be rude not to.) **So should we give gifts to people, even if
their love language isn't gifts?** *(Yes, because they still like to get them.)* **You are right; we
should still give gifts even if we know that the person's love language isn't gifts. Just
like any of the other love languages, we should still love people with them, even if it's
not their love language. I know that if I invited you to my birthday party and you didn't
bring me a gift, I would be really disappointed. Gifts may not be my love language,
but I still like to get them. And one thing that each of you needs to remember is, just
because gifts aren't your love language doesn't mean you won't get gifts, it just means
that you don't feel loved by getting them. You may really like getting gifts but it doesn't
make you feel loved.**

Grade 5 or 6, continue here: Lesson 5.0, Grade 5–6, #2

**"Look at lesson 5.0, #2 and read the directions silently while I read them
aloud."** Have students explain why they think it's not the actual gift that makes
a person feel loved. Call on students to see what they wrote. Tell them to listen
closely to the next part of the lesson and see if their answer is similar to what you
are teaching.

TEACHING/PRESENTATION:

1. What are some special occasions where gifts are involved? *(Birthdays, Christmas, wedding showers, baby showers, Mother's Day, Father's Day, etc.)*

   • Why do we give gifts on days like these? *(To show people that we love them, care, appreciate, celebrate, etc.)*

   • Why is it important to give gifts on these days like these? *(It's cultural and it would be rude not to.)*

AFP: Lesson 5.0, Grade 5–6, #1 & #2

Name _____ Date _____

LESSON 5.0

GIFTS

○ *Makes me feel loved.*
○ *I like it.*

1. Can you remember the best gift you ever received? Describe your gift and explain why you received it:

_____
_____

2. When you get a gift, can that gift itself love you? Think about the definition of loving someone and make an argument explaining why it's not the gift itself that makes a person feel loved:

_____
_____
_____

3. What are the three reasons that a gift makes someone feel loved?

A. _____
B. _____
C. _____

/ /

BRIBERY
HOME CONNECTION SECTION

Bribery is a negative behavior. It means that someone is trying to give a gift to get you to do something or get something from you. You should always ask your parents' permission before receiving a gift. If someone wants to give you a gift and you don't have permission then follow these three simple steps:

A. Politely refuse the gift by saying, "No, thank you." Tell them that your parents don't allow you to take gifts or money without their permission.
B. Tell your parents that someone offered you a gift.
C. If someone in a car tries to offer you a gift to go with them, scream and run away. Try to find help. Do not spend any time talking to them and don't get close to their car.

GRADES 5 & 6

When you get a gift, can that gift love you? *(Rhetorical)* For example, if I buy you a toy, can that toy love you? Before you answer that question, remember what our definition of love is. It's an action word. So I will ask you again, can a toy love you? Can it give you meaningful Words of Affirmation, spend Quality Time with you, or do Acts of Service, intentionally and on its own? *(Expect students to be silly. They will give answers like, "Yes, it can listen to me," or "I can have it say nice things to me." Have students get serious.)* To love people we need to intentionally and deliberately love them on our own using one of the five love languages. Now, I ask again, can a toy love you? *(No)* What I hear you saying is that a toy can't love you. Let's think about that. If a toy can't love you, then what is it about getting a toy that makes some children feel loved? *(Rhetorical)* We have already said that toys can't love us. What do you think it is that makes some children feel loved when they get a gift? *(Call on various students. Answers will vary. The point that they need to get to is it's not the toy that makes them feel loved, it's the person getting the toy for them.)* You're right, the person who gives you the toy is making you feel loved, not the toy itself. Some kids get these mixed up and think it's the toy, when really it's the person giving it. What is it about the person giving the toy that might make them feel loved? *(That they, 1. took their time, 2. spent their money or made it, and most importantly 3. were thinking about them. Write these three things on the board.)*

Grade 5 or 6, continue here: | Lesson 5.0, Grade 5–6, #3

"Look at lesson 5.0, #3, and fill in the lines A, B, C with the reasons I just wrote on the board. You can combine 'spent their money' or 'made it' as one reason for letter B."

Yes, and this is important because people whose love language is gifts feel this way when they get a gift. They may really like the gift, but they feel loved by getting it because they know that the **person** *(point to the board where you wrote the four things, and read)* took their time, spent their money, or made it and were thinking about them. What most people whose love language is Gifts want you to know is that when you give them something, it makes them feel loved because you know them well enough to get them a gift. In other words, you took the time to figure out what they like, you observed what their interests are, and then you took your time to think about them and get it for them. Sometimes people make the mistake of thinking that gift people will only like a gift if it's expensive. This isn't true. Remember, they see a gift as an extension of the giver, so if you give the gift with a good heart, they will usually feel loved by that. That's not to say they don't like expensive gifts! They like virtually all gifts that are given in the right way.

There are some people in our world who will try to convince you that everybody's love language is Gifts. Is that true? *(No!)* The other day I saw a jewelry commercial.

2. We should still give gifts even if it's not the person's love language.

3. If your love language isn't Gifts it doesn't mean you won't get any gifts.

4. Can a gift love you? *(Expect some silly answers and then get class serious.)*

5. Say: To love people we need to intentionally and deliberately love them on our own using one of the five love languages. Can a toy do that?

6. Why do some children feel loved when they get a gift? *(It's the person who gave them the gift who makes them feel loved.)*

7. It makes them feel loved because they took their time, spent their money, and were thinking about them.

8. Gift people want you to know them and their interests.

9. Gifts don't need to be expensive to be good. They need to be meaningful to the receiver.

AFP: Lesson 5.0, Grade 5–6, #3

Name _____ Date _____   **LESSON 5.0**

GIFTS

○ *Makes me feel loved.*
○ *I like it.*

1. Can you remember the best gift you ever received? Describe your gift and explain why you received it:

_____

_____

2. When you get a gift, can that gift itself love you? Think about the definition of loving someone and make an argument explaining why it's not the gift itself that makes a person feel loved:

_____

_____

_____

3. What are the three reasons that a gift makes someone feel loved?

A. _____

B. _____

C. _____

/ /

BRIBERY
HOME CONNECTION SECTION

Bribery is a negative behavior. It means that someone is trying to give a gift to get you to do something or get something from you. You should always ask your parents' permission before receiving a gift. If someone wants to give you a gift and you don't have permission then follow these three simple steps:

A. Politely refuse the gift by saying, "No, thank you." Tell them that your parents don't allow you to take gifts or money without their permission.

B. Tell your parents that someone offered you a gift.

C. If someone in a car tries to offer you a gift to go with them, scream and run away. Try to find help. Do not spend any time talking to them and don't get close to their car.

GRADES 5 & 6

How many of you have seen a jewelry commercial that advertises diamonds, necklaces, etc.? *(Rhetorical)* On this commercial it showed a man giving his wife a diamond necklace and she was so excited about getting it. She told him, "I love you." Then she kissed him. The commercial said, "Show her that you really love her, get her diamonds." What this commercial is trying to say is that she will feel loved by him if he gets her diamonds. We have already said that not everybody feels loved when they get gifts, right? *(Right)* So why does this jewelry company want people to think that everybody's love language is Gifts? *(So they can sell you jewelry.)* Right, if everybody thinks this, then they will go out and buy diamonds, and the company will make money. Very sneaky, but you won't be caught off guard, because you have figured out that not everybody feels loved when you buy something for them. Now, that doesn't mean they won't really like getting a diamond from you, but there's a chance that it might not make them feel loved. This is true for any gift that you get, not just diamonds. Appreciating and being thankful for what you get is very different from feeling loved.

How many of you have bought something for a relative who said, "Oh you didn't need to do that. I'd rather you had just made me a card"? See, their love language is probably what? *(Words of Affirmation)* Having nice things said to them is what makes them feel loved. If you were to buy them a gift, you definitely would want to include a card. Getting to know people and being a good detective is what will help you become great at loving people. In the example that I just gave, the person said they liked getting cards, and cards usually have nice words in them. By picking up on these clues you can learn how to love people. It works the same way with gift people. You have to get to know them and figure out what they like. Look at what they already own, what they like to eat, or what they are interested in. Be a good listener and ask them about their life. One of my favorite questions to ask is, "What is your favorite color?" I know that this information might come in handy someday when I'm getting them a gift. Gift people like to get gifts because it makes them feel loved, and we should get them gifts more often than just special occasions. I have a friend who loves Cheetos. She is a Gift person, so every once in a while I buy her a bag of Cheetos and leave it in her office as a surprise. When you get a gift for someone, it doesn't have to be big or expensive. Gifts can be made or found. If you know someone who likes rocks and collects them, you could try to find a really awesome rock. Use your knowledge about the person, plus imagination, and try to get them something that they will like.

Some people are afraid to tell others that their love language is Gifts. They think that if they tell someone, the person may think that they are greedy or selfish. If your love language is Gifts then you should be proud of it. Each love language is equal to all of the others. If people don't understand about gifts being your love language, then take the time to teach them. Most people won't be trained like you are. Always be proud of your love language.

10. Commercials sometimes try to convince us that everybody's love language is Gifts.

11. Why would companies try to convince people that everyone has the love language of Gifts? *(to sell products)*

12. In order to figure out what a person wants for a gift we need to be good detectives. This involves asking questions about their life and being observant.

13. Gift people like to get gifts because it makes them feel loved. We should get them gifts often.

14. A gift can be something small, inexpensive, or handmade, as long as it has meaning.

15. Some people are afraid to tell others that their love language is Gifts because they worry that people will think they are greedy or selfish.

16. Everyone should be proud of their love language. All love languages are equal.

[TRANSITION TO OPPOSITE]

ANTICIPATORY SET:

Some people give gifts to make others feel loved. When we give gifts to make people feel loved, appreciated, celebrated, happy, or just to be nice, we are doing it with the right motivation, and this is good. Sometimes however, people give gifts for different reasons, and those motivations are not good.

TEACHING/PRESENTATION:

Most of the time when we receive a gift, we think, "Wow, that was really nice," and it makes us grateful. We usually know the person, and we understand why they are giving us the gift—especially if it's our birthday or some other special occasion when giving and receiving gifts is expected. But what would you think about someone who offered you a really cool gift for no reason? Let's say this is a person you don't know very well, and they offered you money or a cool video game and you knew that it was a lot of money or really expensive. **Would you be suspicious?** *(yes)* **Why?** *(Don't know him, makes me wonder why, seems weird, etc.)* **Yes, it should make you suspicious if you don't know them or can't think of a good reason why they would want to give you something.** *[Keep in mind that this is building the foundation for the "Touch" lesson that will connect bribery with "Don't tell anyone."]*

Some people give gifts so they can get something in return. They aren't really giving a gift to be nice. It seems like they are being nice, but they are actually giving a gift to get something from you. We call this negative behavior "bribery." Bribery is bad because it comes with a false motive or what is called an "ulterior motive." The person is secretly thinking that if they give you a gift then you will think they are nice and give them something in return or do something for them. They may not ask you to do or give anything at first, but eventually they will. If you refuse to do what they want, then they may try to make you feel guilty and remind you that they gave you something.

Some examples of bribery could include a student who is trying to "buy" your friendship with a gift; a friend or family member who doesn't want you to tell on them, so they give you something so you won't say anything; or a stranger who offers you something so you will go somewhere with them. And I'm sure we could think of a lot more examples. Of course if this happens to you, I want you to have some strategies to deal with it. Here are three ways to deal with bribery:

1. Politely refuse to take the gift by saying, "No, thank you." Tell them that your parents don't like you to take gifts or money from anyone without their permission.

[TRANSITION TO OPPOSITE]

ANTICIPATORY SET:

1. Some people give gifts for reasons that aren't good.

TEACHING/PRESENTATION:

1. We need to be suspicious of gifts given by strangers without any apparent reason.

2. When people give us a gift and have a false motive or "ulterior motive" this negative behavior is call "bribery."

3. People give bribes to influence the decisions of others. They may do it to:
   • buy friendship
   • keep you from telling about something they did
   • an adult/teenager might try to get you to go with them or do something for them

4. There are four strategies that you need to learn in case someone tries to bribe you:
   • Politely refuse to take the gift by saying, "No, thank you." Tell them your parents don't like you to take gifts or money from anyone without their permission.
   • Tell your parents that someone offered you a gift and you felt uncomfortable about it. See what they think.
   • If it happens at school, tell a teacher or other adult and then tell your parents when you get home.
   • If an adult/teenager offers you something to get into a car or go somewhere with them, scream and run away. Try to find help. Do not spend any time talking to them, and don't get close to their car.

5. If something doesn't seem right, always ask your parents about it.

2. Tell your parents that someone offered you a gift and you felt weird about it. See what they think.

3. If an adult offers you something to get into a car or go somewhere with them, scream and run away. Try to find help. Do not spend any time talking to them, and don't get close to their car.

When you get those feelings that something isn't right, always check it out with your parents. Remember that it's okay to politely refuse a gift. The good news is most of the time people have good motives and are just trying to be nice. If everything is good, your parents won't have a problem with you receiving a gift after they give you permission.

Grades 1–6	Lesson 5.0, Grades 1–6, Bottom of the page

Have students role-play "gift refusal" using the three ways to deal with bribery. Have students take turns offering gifts and refusing. The three things to do are written at the bottom of their page. For fun you could have three in a group and one be the parent or guardian they report to. The primary focus for this activity is number 1 or "A" on their sheet. I would suggest for the third one you simply discuss "screaming and running away," otherwise you will have a classroom of chaos.

CLOSURE:

Today we learned about the love language called Gifts. Some people feel loved when they receive gifts. Most everybody really likes to get gifts because it makes them feel special and appreciated. Holidays, birthdays, and other occasions are a time for people to give and receive gifts. Even if someone's love language isn't Gifts, it's still important to give them one when the time is right. If someone's love language is Gifts, then we should try to get them gifts more often than we would for others. The gifts we get them should reflect their interests. We get to know what they would like by being a good listener and asking them questions about their life. When people receive gifts they see the gift as an extension of the one who gave it. A gift becomes a symbol that can represent appreciation, value, sacrifice, love, devotion, apologies, celebration, etc. It is more than just a material item or thing.

When people use Gifts to get something in return, we call this negative behavior bribery. Bribery means that the gift giver has an ulterior motive for giving the gift. If someone tries to bribe you or you think that they might be, you should:

1. Politely refuse the gift.

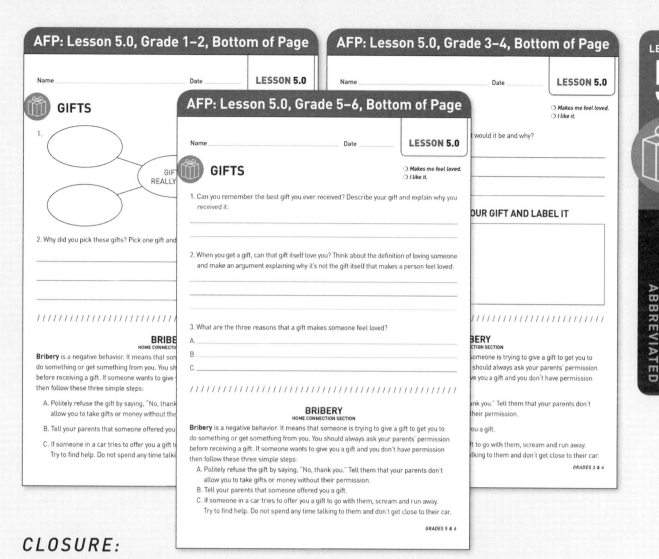

AFP: Lesson 5.0, Grade 1–2, Bottom of Page

Name _____ Date _____ **LESSON 5.0**

GIFTS

1.

(GIF... / REALLY...)

2. Why did you pick these gifts? Pick one gift and...

_____

_____

///////////////////////////////////

BRIBE...
HOME CONNECTION...

Bribery is a negative behavior. It means that so...
do something or get something from you. You sh...
before receiving a gift. If someone wants to give...
then follow these three simple steps:

A. Politely refuse the gift by saying, "No, than...
allow you to take gifts or money without the...

B. Tell your parents that someone offered you...

C. If someone in a car tries to offer you a gift t...
Try to find help. Do not spend any time talki...

AFP: Lesson 5.0, Grade 3–4, Bottom of Page

Name _____ Date _____ **LESSON 5.0**

○ *Makes me feel loved.*
○ *I like it.*

... would it be and why?

_____

...UR GIFT AND LABEL IT

///////////////////////////////////

...BERY
...TION SECTION

...someone is trying to give a gift to get you to
...should always ask your parents' permission
...ve you a gift and you don't have permission

...nk you." Tell them that your parents don't
...their permission.

...you a gift.

...ft to go with them, scream and run away.
...lking to them and don't get close to their car.

GRADES 3 & 4

AFP: Lesson 5.0, Grade 5–6, Bottom of Page

Name _____ Date _____ **LESSON 5.0**

GIFTS

○ *Makes me feel loved.*
○ *I like it.*

1. Can you remember the best gift you ever received? Describe your gift and explain why you received it:

_____

2. When you get a gift, can that gift itself love you? Think about the definition of loving someone and make an argument explaining why it's not the gift itself that makes a person feel loved:

_____

_____

3. What are the three reasons that a gift makes someone feel loved?

A. _____

B. _____

C. _____

///

BRIBERY
HOME CONNECTION SECTION

Bribery is a negative behavior. It means that someone is trying to give a gift to get you to do something or get something from you. You should always ask your parents' permission before receiving a gift. If someone wants to give you a gift and you don't have permission then follow these three simple steps:

A. Politely refuse the gift by saying, "No, thank you." Tell them that your parents don't allow you to take gifts or money without their permission.

B. Tell your parents that someone offered you a gift.

C. If someone in a car tries to offer you a gift to go with them, scream and run away. Try to find help. Do not spend any time talking to them and don't get close to their car.

GRADES 5 & 6

CLOSURE:

Today we learned about the love language called Gifts. Some people feel loved when they receive gifts. Most everybody likes to get gifts because it makes them feel special and appreciated. Holidays, birthdays, and other occasions are a time for people to give and receive gifts. Even if someone's love language isn't Gifts, it's still important to give them one when the time is right. If someone's love language is Gifts, then we should try to get them gifts more often than we would for others. The gifts we get them should reflect their interests. We get to know what they would like by being a good listener and asking them questions about their life. When people receive gifts, they see the gift as an extension of the one who gave it. A gift becomes a symbol that can represent appreciation, value, sacrifice, love, devotion, apologies, celebration, etc. It is more than just a material item or thing.

When people use gifts to get something in return, we call this negative behavior bribery. Bribery means the gift giver has an ulterior motive for giving the gift. If someone tries to bribe you, you should:

1. **Politely refuse the gift.**

2. **Tell your parents.**

3. **Tell an adult at school.**

4. **In the rare case where an adult may be trying to get you to go somewhere with them, scream, run away, don't talk to them, and find help.**

Ask yourself, "Do Gifts make me feel loved, or do I just really like to receive them?" Please fill in a circle by one of the items at the top right-hand side of your Academic Focus Page. The items say, "Makes me feel loved," or "I like it."

Let's take a look at the assignment.

INDEPENDENT PRACTICE/ASSIGNMENT:

Each student will talk to their family and record the following information on paper:

1. Each student will interview their family members and try to figure out what a gift means to them.

2. They will ask their family to describe what a really good gift looks like.

3. See if they can draw any conclusions about their families' love languages.

4. Tell the students when you will return to teach the next lesson. Remind them that you will be asking various students about their experience the next time you teach the love languages.

5. Review the objectives on the white board. Have students talk for a few seconds with each other about how well they learned the subject. Ask if anyone needs questions answered.

2. **Tell your parents.**

3. **Tell an adult at school.**

4. **In the rare case where an adult may be trying to get you to go somewhere with them, scream, run away, don't talk to them, and find help.**

Grades 1–6	Lesson 5.0, Grades 1–6, Bottom of the page

Have students role-play "gift refusal" using the three ways to deal with bribery. Have students take turns offering gifts and refusing. The three things to do are written at the bottom of their page. For fun you could have three in a group and one be the parent or guardian that they report to. The primary focus for this activity is number 1 or "A" on their sheet. I would suggest for the third one you simply discuss "screaming and running away;" otherwise you will have a classroom of chaos.

Ask yourself, "Do gifts make me feel loved, or do I just really like to receive them?" Please fill in a circle by one of the items at the top right-hand side of your Academic Focus Page. The items say, "Makes me feel loved," or "I like it."

Let's take a look at the assignment.

INDEPENDENT PRACTICE/ASSIGNMENT:

Each student will talk to their family and record the following information on paper:

1. Each student will interview their family members and try to figure out what a gift means to them.

2. They will ask their family to describe what a really good gift looks like.

3. See if they can draw any conclusions about their families' love languages.

4. Tell the students when you will return to teach the next lesson. Remind them that you will be asking various students about their experience the next time you teach the love languages.

5. Review the objectives on the white board. Have students talk for a few seconds with each other about how well they learned the subject. Ask if anyone needs questions answered.

FINAL THOUGHTS

I have worked at schools where a child feels lucky if he receives one or two gifts for Christmas. I have worked at other schools where the extravagance was so great that a child couldn't remember everything he received for Christmas. Both of these situations play into how a child feels if his/her love language is Gifts.

We talk a lot about poverty and its impact on the family. The newspapers and educational reports make it clear that there is a definite link between poverty levels and school failures. But when was the last time you heard a report about how kids feel because they're poor? I think about what it must be like for the child whose love language is Gifts but who doesn't receive any. How do they cope? Do they feel less loved because the gifts are so far and few between? Do they seek other avenues to fill those needs? Do negative behaviors increase for lack of feeling loved? Perhaps love plays a bigger role in poor behavior than we think.

We talk a lot about wealth and getting ahead. Is the child with it all truly better off? Truly more loved? If Gifts are his/her love language and they can't remember them all because there are so many, is that healthy? Does it create anxiety because of the uncertainty of which gifts are to be valued and which ones are to be thought of as ordinary? Does an abundance of gifts create suspicion that none of them represent love but all are simply surplus? Do negative behaviors increase for lack of feeling loved? Perhaps lack of love plays a bigger role in poor behavior than we think, even for children who are well off.

Learning the love languages allows individuals an opportunity to discover what motivates them in key areas. With personal discovery comes a freedom to realize better choices. Discovering the love language known as Gifts is one more step in the right direction.

FROM THE CLASSROOM

A third grade boy came into my office one day. He was very upset about something that had happened. He said, "Mr. Freed, you know how you taught about Gifts last week?"

I said, "Yes."

He said, "Well, I gave another boy a really cool necklace that I bought for his birthday with my own money, and he gave it to someone else."

"Wow!" I said. "That wasn't very nice. Why did he do that?"

He shrugged his shoulders, and I asked if he wanted me to set up a meeting between him and the other boy, to which he agreed.

The two boys met together that afternoon and began to talk it out. I asked the birthday boy if he received a necklace from him.

He said, "Yes!" with a smile on his face. I said quietly, "Did you give a necklace to another boy in this school?"

He said "Yes!" I became confused. The look on his face was that of pride.

He reached into his shirt and pulled the birthday necklace out and said, "See, I kept the necklace you bought for me. I'm a gift person, and I liked it a lot better than the one I bought for myself the day before my birthday. My mom and I were surprised that you knew me well enough to know what kind of necklace I would want. I gave my necklace to John because he's a gift person too. He doesn't have very many nice things."

We wrapped up the conversation with talk about other gifts the boy had received, and the two of them left my office feeling a lot better. I sat there with a smile on my face knowing that the lesson had impacted three lives.

CHAPTER 7

Safe Touch

INTRODUCTION

No other love language has been more distorted than "Touch." I suppose this is partly due to the confusion it causes when it's done wrong. Regardless of your opinion concerning touch, we should all be able to agree that everyone is hardwired to receive it. During this introduction we need to freely consider this love language, so that you as an educator can become comfortable addressing it. This becomes especially important if your responsibility includes teaching children how to deal with or avoid the unsafe touch, which of course falls under the category of "child abuse." If you are uncomfortable with this topic, your students will be as well. Your students should feel comfortable confiding in you regarding any personal safety issue. We as educators are often their first line of defense.

One of my goals is to help you face your fears, doubts, and concerns, and look at touch from a practical point of view. If you are worried that I'm going to have you hug every student whose love language is Touch, then please know your worries are unwarranted. If you think I'm going to place you in some legally unsafe territory, again you would be wrong. What I am going to do is talk to you honestly about the subject of touch as it relates to the love languages and how we as educators need to interact within it. I wish to give you the tools to love those students who have the love language of Touch, as well as empower all others to do the same. This may come as a surprise, but after students understand touch as a love language, they are less likely to initiate physical contact with educators who do not desire touch. Having open and honest discussions with students promotes health and happiness. Let's start with some basics.

Human beings have trillions of nerve cells. Our bodies from the time of birth cry out for touch. There is much evidence to show that infants who are not touched are more likely to be physically and mentally delayed than others their same age. In some instances, babies who received very little touch actually died. We can conclude that touch is crucial for a healthy existence. Babies and children inherently understand their need for touch and will seek it. This explains one of the reasons babies stop crying when they are picked up. Although this concept is basic, it's important to understand that children don't leave their need for touch at home when they start school.

During the first years in their home, children may have been held, hugged, and kissed freely. As children start school they discover that touch has parameters. For most students this creates no problems as they begin to understand social norms, but for some there's a deep sense of loss. This loss can be difficult for children to articulate, and they may well react to it in a variety of negative ways. For some students, being whiny, needy, or fictitiously injured can become a subtle or not-so-subtle replacement. If this is never addressed, these same students may go on to upper grade levels bringing their behaviors with them. Helping students understand the love language of Touch can be very beneficial in alleviating these problems. Like all of the love languages, the benefit of understanding what makes us feel loved can also give us insight into poor behaviors which we believe will make us feel loved.

Because children come hardwired for different levels of touch, all educators have to decide how they are going to deal with this subject. Many male and female educators have decided that the safest route is a "no contact" policy. Their reasoning is, "If I don't touch anyone, I can't be accused of anything." Being a male educator, I can fully understand and appreciate why some have chosen this route. Unfortunately, this "no contact" approach doesn't address the needs of students whose love language is touch. If you reside in this camp, let me explain why this is an out-of-balance approach and detrimental to your students.

When educators choose to use the "no contact" policy as their dogmatic theme, it robs the classroom and the educator of a warm/friendly environment. Touch used appropriately helps students make connections with their teacher and motivates them to perform. This is especially true for those whose love language is Touch. To withhold touch is the equivalent of withholding any other love language. Regardless of how uncomfortable we are with touch, we must find some way within our power to create connections with those whose love language is Touch.

Touch does not have to be complicated nor questionable. Educators need not fear appropriate touch. The last time I checked, nobody was going to prison because they shook a student's hand or high-fived them gently. What I'm getting at here is if you are a non-touch person, using either of these techniques is sufficient to make safe touch connections with students.

As you have learned by now, one size does not fit all when it comes to love languages. Not everyone feels like being touched, or if they do it may not be you that they want to be touched by. There are a variety of reasons why students may or may not want you to have physical contact with them. I am now speaking to those of you who are in the "we can't get enough hugs" camp. Some teachers are very comfortable with touch, but unfortunately their students aren't. Teachers can inappropriately cross the line with any student when they enter into their personal space without permission. I have witnessed teachers giving children hugs under the belief that "all" children like hugs. This is not the case. Educators must be careful not to encroach on students' space without their permission. This is why teaching the love language of Touch is important. When you teach this and the final lesson, it creates discussion about who is and who isn't comfortable with touch. This is a good time for you to tell students how you feel about touch. If you are not a touch person, tell them. If you are, tell them. Either way, let them know what you are comfortable with, and they will learn how to approach you. I'm not a touch person, and I explain to my students that I don't care for hugs. I tell them I will high-five them on occasion or pat them on the back but beyond that I'm not comfortable. I ask them if they are able to respect my comfort level. I have yet to have any student say no.

The opposite of Safe Touch is, of course, unsafe touch. There have been countless curriculums written on this subject. Educational institutions and other agencies have taken it upon themselves to ensure that children won't fall victim to these crimes. I have read over many of the available curriculums and have managed to come up with yet another version/lesson (my own) to help children be safe. Teachers and parents have applauded my lesson because it is balanced. Students who are taught this lesson get the whole picture rather than just a piece of it. Because students are used to looking for the opposite of any love language, transitioning is easy for them.

It is highly probable that there is a curriculum in place at your school that addresses the subject of child abuse. If this is the case, then the second half of this lesson can simply be used as a refresher or not used at all. Here are ten key reminders when teaching any lesson on child abuse:

1. Inform the class that you will be discussing an issue that requires everyone's serious side.
2. Use appropriate humor when you can, to show students that you are comfortable with the topic. The beauty of this love language lesson is that it creates a better balance when transitioning to the topic of child abuse after the first half of the lesson.
3. Let students know that touch is a good thing and we are all wired for it.
4. Set ground rules before teaching the lesson. "We don't use names in this class when telling stories. If you have a story you would like to share, I would like to hear it later in private."
5. Be honest and straightforward. The truth is this is not comfortable dinner table conversation. Students need to know that just because something is not

comfortable does not mean it is not important to talk about.

6. Understand child abuse statistics. A large percentage of abuse occurs by relatives who are married, not single. Challenge some of your pre-conceived notions (if you have any) about what an abuser looks like.

7. Let students know it is very unlikely it will happen to them, but if it has or does, you want them to know what to do. Your job is not to create panic and paranoia but rather to inform and educate. Your calm attitude will take you a long way when it comes to students confiding with you. If students sense that you are uncomfortable with the topic, they will not want to talk to you. They are most likely already uncomfortable with the topic or they would have said something earlier.

8. Know your school's follow-up procedures for students who disclose. I have yet to work in a school where the principal wasn't involved or informed of abuse reports.

9. If you think a student is going to disclose some type of abuse to you, get others involved. If you have a school counselor, ask the student if it would be all right to include them during your conversation. If you get into a conversation and it turns to disclosure, try to stop the conversation and get the counselor or another designated person on board. Don't ask the student a lot of questions. If it turns out to be a true criminal case, your questions could be used to have the case thrown out. Many an abuse case has been thrown out due to a "leading questions" defense. Leave questioning to authorities who have a prescribed way of asking children questions.

10. Never promise confidentiality. All states require that educators report child abuse. Report all situations to an administrator even if you don't think it's that big a deal. They may know things about the student's past that you don't.

If you have made it this far, you are ready to teach the lesson. I think you will enjoy the way that it is structured. I found three pictures helpful when teaching the students. The first picture is that of a baby in diapers. The second picture is that of a doctor listening with a stethoscope to a child breathing. The third picture is of two children in swimsuits (boy and girl) with the girl wearing a two-piece. These pictures aren't necessary but are helpful as visuals. The children's swimsuit picture makes it easier because many elementary girls may not think of the chest area as being private. A visual of the two-piece swimsuit takes care of this problem when you describe in the lesson "any place your swimsuit covers."

If taught correctly, your students should be able to walk away feeling they know what to do for themselves and friends. They should not be paranoid or in a state of panic. They should have laughed some before the lesson is over. When was the last time you and your students laughed when teaching a lesson on "Child Abuse"? Enjoy this unique approach!

LESSON 6
TOUCH
(SCRIPTED)

OBJECTIVE:

Students will be able to understand and describe the love language known as Touch. They will understand the concepts of appropriate touch, uncomfortable but necessary touch, and inappropriate or unsafe touch. They will have a working knowledge of what to do if they or a friend are the victim of inappropriate/unsafe touch (child abuse).

Write on white board:

1. I can describe the difference between safe touch and unsafe touch.
2. I know what to do if someone touches me or someone I know in an unsafe way.

(Have students talk with each other for thirty seconds about what they think they are going to be learning today.)

REVIEW:

Instructor will ask volunteer students to explain:

1. What are the two goals for teaching the love languages? *(To learn your own love languages and to be able to identify the love languages of others.)*
2. What was the last love language that was taught? *(Gifts)*
3. Review the last lesson's objectives that you wrote on the white board.
4. What makes a good gift? *(An item that reflects the interests of the person.)*
5. Can gifts have more meaning than just being an item? *(Yes, they become an extension of the person giving it. They can be a symbol that represents love, devotion, apologies, celebration, etc.)*
6. What is considered a negative behavior that is opposite of Gifts? *(Bribery)*
7. What is bribery? *(Giving someone a gift with a false or ulterior motive. They want something in return.)*
8. Call on a few volunteer students to quickly discuss how their assignment went and what they experienced.
9. Remind students that each time they learn a love language you want them to ask themselves: Does this love language make me feel loved, or do I just like it?

LESSON 6
TOUCH
(ABBREVIATED)

OBJECTIVE:

Students will be able to understand and describe the love language known as Touch. They will understand the concepts of appropriate touch, uncomfortable but necessary touch, and inappropriate or unsafe touch. They will have a working knowledge of what to do if they or a friend are the victim of inappropriate/unsafe touch (child abuse).

Write on white board:

1. I can describe the difference between safe touch and unsafe touch.
2. I know what to do if someone touches me or someone I know in an unsafe way.

(Have students talk with each other for thirty seconds about what they think they are going to be learning today.)

REVIEW:

Instructor will ask volunteer students to explain:

1. What are the two goals for teaching the love languages? *(To learn your own love languages and to be able to identify the love languages of others.)*
2. What was the last love language that was taught? *(Gifts)*
3. Review the last lesson's objectives that you wrote on the white board.
4. What makes a good gift? *(An item that reflects the interests of the person.)*
5. Can gifts have more meaning than just being an item? *(Yes, they become an extension of the person giving it. They can be a symbol that represents love, devotion, apologies, celebration, etc.)*
6. What is considered a negative behavior that is opposite of Gifts? *(Bribery)*
7. What is bribery? *(Giving someone a gift with a false or ulterior motive. They want something in return.)*
8. Call on a few volunteer students to quickly discuss how their assignment went and what they experienced.
9. Remind students that each time they learn a love language you want them to ask themselves: Does this love language make me feel loved, or do I just like it?

ANTICIPATORY SET:

Today we will be learning about the last love language called Touch. *(Write Touch on the board.)* **Like all of the love languages, some people, not all, feel really loved through touch. Touch may or may not be your love language, but it is important for health and survival. Our bodies are made up of trillions of nerve cells, and they love to be touched by others. Here's an experiment you can do to prove my point we have all been wired for touch by others. Try this: Try to tickle your ribs.** *(Demonstrate tickling your ribs.)* **Isn't it weird that when you tickle your ribs it doesn't really tickle, but it really tickles when someone else does it to you? And getting your back scratched always feels better when someone else does it. There is something about being touched by someone else that makes it better. Let's find out if Touch is your love language.**

TEACHING/PRESENTATION:

Grade 3 or 4, start here:	Lesson 6.0, Grade 3–4, #1

"Take out some colored pencils. We are now going to do activity #1 on your 6.0 lesson. Follow along silently as I read the direction to you." This lesson provides a visual connection for students to see who they connect with. They will be surprised where most of the lines go or don't go. This is a great opportunity for you as the educator to evaluate the amount of connection your student perceives he/she is getting. Some students don't have a lot of family. Reinforce the idea that if they don't have a lot of lines or family this is perfectly okay.

Grade 5 or 6, start here:	Lesson 6.0, Grade 5–6, #1

"We are now going to answer question #1 on your 6.0 lesson. Follow along silently as I read the direction to you." Have students write a few sentences predicting why they believe touch is required for a baby to be healthy. After students finish this question have some volunteers tell the class why they think it's important. Ask them to listen closely to see if their answer was close. If their reason wasn't listed, you could encourage them to look up facts online (with permission) regarding this topic.

From the first day you were born you came with the need for touch. When a little tiny baby doesn't get touched, what do they do? *(They cry)* **That's right, they cry!** *[I usually make a crying baby sound for effect—optional]* **They hear or smell somebody close by, and**

ANTICIPATORY SET:

1. Introduce the love language of Touch. *(Write "touch" on the board.)*

2. Touch is important for health.

3. Bodies are made up of trillions of nerve cells.

4. We have been wired for touch by others. *(Tickle their own ribs, exercise)*

TEACHING/PRESENTATION:

Start with:

1. **Academic Focus Pages:**
   • **Academic Focus Page [Lesson 6.0, Grade 3–4, #1]**
   • **Academic Focus Page [Lesson 6.0, Grade 5–6, #1]**

AFP: Lesson 6.0, Grade 3–4, #1

Name _____ Date _____ **LESSON 6.0**

SAFE TOUCH

○ *Makes me feel loved.*
○ *I like it.*

WHO CONNECTS WITH YOU?

1. Draw a line from a type of touch on the left to the people who connect with you using that touch on the right. You may be surprised that some of these are considered touch. It's okay if you don't have a lot of lines; everyone is different.

HINT: Use a different colored pencil for each box of people.

Hug / Kiss on the cheek / Back rub / Foot rub / Pat on the back / Snuggling / Wrestling / High five / Head rub / Sitting close / Holding hands

GRANDFATHER GRANDMOTHER
BROTHER SISTER
DAD MOM
AUNT UNCLE
OTHER RELATIVE OR FRIEND

WHAT IS APPROPRIATE?

2. From the list of touches above, write the ones you think would be appropriate at school. If the teacher were to ask you, "Why do you think the touches you chose are appropriate at school?" could you support your answers with evidence that makes sense?

_____

///

HOME CONNECTION SECTION

Everybody has a different comfort level when it comes to touch. Some people like to be touched and some people don't. Some people only like certain people to touch them. All people have a right to choose what their comfort level is. We need to be respectful of a person's personal space, even if their love language is Touch.

GRADES 3 & 4

AFP: Lesson 6.0, Grade 5–6, #1

Name _____ Date _____ **LESSON 6.0**

SAFE TOUCH

○ *Makes me feel loved.*
○ *I like it.*

1. Thinking deeper: We know that babies require touch to be healthy, but why? Write your best prediction for why you believe touch is required for a baby to be healthy. Use scientific examples if you know of any.

_____

2. Thinking about different cultures and different styles: What are some ways that you have observed people greeting each other or celebrating an accomplishment? For example, I've seen people give high fives after they make a goal playing soccer. Now it's your turn:

_____

3. Obviously the way you use touch at home with your family or during sports is a lot different than when you are at school. List as many ways that you can think of that would be appropriate or considered safe touch at school. Your school rules should help you with the answers:

_____

Everybody has a different comfort level when it comes to touch. Some people like to be touched and some people don't. Some people only like certain people to touch them. All people have a right to choose what their comfort level is. We need to be respectful of a person's personal space even if their love language is Touch.

GRADES 5 & 6

they cry until they get picked up. Of course we know that babies cry for other reasons, but sometimes they cry simply because they want to be held. Did you know that a baby who doesn't get held very often may not develop right? Babies need to be held and loved through touch so they can grow up to have healthy brains and bodies. Touch sends signals to the baby that everything is okay, and this relaxes them and they can sleep better. There are some studies that show their brain development improves—probably because they are calmer and sleep better. This is just one of many things that a baby benefits from through touch. Ah, the life of a baby.

As babies get older and become toddlers, they still like to be held. How many of you have younger brothers or sisters who are two or three and still like to be held? *[Asked to keep students tracking]* Sometimes toddlers get big, and it gets harder to carry them for a long time. Parents are usually happy the toddlers have learned to walk so they don't have to keep carrying them. But lots of times you will see a toddler climb up into his parent's lap and be happy as a clam. And this is true for some older kids too. Some of you in here come from families that are very physical, and there's lots of touch in your home. Your parents are always hugging you, kissing you on top of your head, or scratching your backs. In your home, touch is a way of life.

Not all families are into touch that much. Some families only hug each other once in a while, or they only kiss each other goodbye. This isn't bad, it's just their way. Each family has its own way of showing love through touch. The only time this becomes a problem is if your love language is Touch and you come from a family that doesn't touch each other that much. For those of you who fit this category, you may have to talk to your parents about your love language and ask them to give you more hugs. One good strategy is to hug your mom or dad once in a while when you come home from school. Usually you can get them into the habit, and they will start hugging you back. If they ask you why you are hugging them, you can tell them because that's your love language and explain it to them. Not all parents feel comfortable hugging their children. Dads may or may not be that huggy, but I guarantee that when their son or daughter hugs them usually their heart will melt.

Have you ever noticed that as boys and girls get older they tend to relate to their best friends differently when it comes to touch? Let me give you an example. In middle school or high school you may see two girls who give each other a really big hug when they first see each other in the morning. *[I pretend I'm hugging another girl and of course put on a big show like I haven't seen them forever. I'm overly dramatic. The kids love it!]* They act like they haven't seen each other for years when they probably just saw each other the day before. On the other hand I can pretty much guarantee you that you will not usually see a boy run up to another boy and give him a big embracing hug in school. *[I act like I'm hugging another boy like I did when I pretended to hug like girls, and the*

2. From the first day you were born you came with the need for touch.

3. Discuss why babies need touch.

4. As babies get older and become toddlers, they still like to be held.

5. Some of you come from homes where there is lots of touch.

6. Not all families are into touch that much.

7. Each family has its own level of touch.

8. Lack of touch becomes a problem if your love language is Touch.
   • Talk to your parents and explain about your love language.
   • Give your parents hugs, and hopefully they will hug you back.

9. As they get older, boys and girls relate to their best friends differently when it comes to touch.

10. Middle school examples of best friends meeting each other in the morning.
   (Teacher acts out scenarios with imaginary people.)

whole class will be laughing.] **Usually when guys hug, they do what I call the "guy hug."
It looks more like a greeting where they grab hands like they're going to arm wrestle
and then very quickly move toward each other and back. It's not really a hug at all.** *(I
usually demonstrate it with a pretend person.)* **Boys and girls tend to express touch very
differently as they get older. Have you ever wondered why boys like to wrestle around
so much? It's because that's one of the ways they get their touch. Boys and some girls
love to wrestle with their brothers, friends, or parents. They love contact sports like
football, hockey, and of course wrestling. All of these sports are ways they engage in
touch, and it's usually not gentle. Some of the girls in here probably have brothers who
want to wrestle all of the time. Some boys in here might have gotten in trouble because
they wrestle too much and at a place where they aren't supposed to, like in the house
or on the playground!**

**Here is another interesting fact about touch: In the United States we usually greet
people with a handshake, but in other countries their customs may be very different.
In other words some countries deal with touch a lot differently from the way we do.
For example, in many European countries, such as France, they may greet visitors with
a kiss to both sides of the face. In other countries, like Japan, they may simply bow.**
[I usually demonstrate both of these examples with an imaginary person.] **If you travel or
meet someone from another country, it is very possible that their culture and customs
are different from yours. We always need to be respectful and try to honor the customs
and cultures of other people.**

Grade 5 or 6, continue here:	Lesson 6.0, Grade 5–6, #2

**"We are now going to answer question #2 on your 6.0 lesson. Follow along
silently as I read the direction to you."** Have students answer the question
by writing a few examples of greetings and celebrations. When the students
complete their written work, have volunteers come up to the front and
demonstrate a greeting or a celebration with a friend they listed. There is usually
a lot of laughs with this activity.

**Touch is a really great thing, and some people feel loved through touch. If you
really like to be close to people and it makes you feel loved, then touch is probably your
love language. If you don't really care much for touch and just like the occasional hug
or your back scratched, then you probably just like touch and it's most likely not your
love language. People whose love language is touch love to be close to parents and
others frequently. They usually love hugs and kisses, back rubs, and snuggling. All of
these things make them feel loved. Most of the people I know who feel loved through
touch have no doubt that this is their love language. It's usually quite obvious to them.**

11. Boys and girls tend to express touch differently when they get older.
   • Boys and some girls like to wrestle and participate in contact sports.
   • Boys tend to get in trouble if they wrestle in places like house or on playground.

12. Culture: In the U.S. we shake hands as a greeting.

13. Other countries deal with touch differently.
   • France—kiss to both sides of face
   • Japan—bowing

14. Always respect other cultures.
   • **Academic Focus Page [Lesson 6.0, Grade 5–6, #2]**

AFP: Lesson 6.0, Grade 5–6, #2

Name _____ Date _____ | **LESSON 6.0**

SAFE TOUCH

○ *Makes me feel loved.*
○ *I like it.*

1. Thinking deeper: We know that babies require touch to be healthy, but why? Write your best prediction for why you believe touch is required for a baby to be healthy. Use scientific examples if you know of any.

_____
_____
_____
_____

2. Thinking about different cultures and different styles: What are some ways that you have observed people greeting each other or celebrating an accomplishment? For example, I've seen people give high fives after they make a goal playing soccer. Now it's your turn:

_____
_____
_____
_____

3. Obviously the way you use touch at home with your family or during sports is a lot different than when you are at school. List as many ways that you can think of that would be appropriate or considered safe touch at school. Your school rules should help you with the answers:

_____
_____
_____

Everybody has a different comfort level when it comes to touch. Some people like to be touched and some people don't. Some people only like certain people to touch them. All people have a right to choose what their comfort level is. We need to be respectful of a person's personal space even if their love language is Touch.

GRADES 5 & 6

Everybody has different comfort levels when it comes to touch. Some people like to be touched, and some people don't. Some people only like certain people to touch them, and that's okay. That is their right. We need to be respectful of people's personal space whether Touch is their love language or not. Remember when we talked about drawing our personal safety line? *(Wait for responses and remind students what drawing their personal safety line looks like.)* Sometimes we have to do this when someone invades our personal space by touching us. They may not know that we don't like what they are doing. As your teacher, *[This is where you will explain whether you are a touch person or not and how you want students to approach you. Set clear guidelines regarding what is acceptable to you. Ask the class if they can respect your personal space. This will be your line drawn and a reference point to gently remind a student should they cross it in the future.]* I will always try to respect your personal space, and if you don't like something that I do please politely tell me.

Grade 1 or 2, continue here: Lesson 6.0, Grade 1–2, #1 & #2

"We are now going to do exercise #1 and #2 on your 6.0 lesson. Follow along silently as I read the direction to you." Have students fill in the ovals with different people they allow in their space. The teacher should guide students by reading each oval and having students write mom, dad, friend, etc. This Academic Focus Page has been designed so a teacher can make reference to it in the future when students invade the space of other students. For example, a teacher can say, "Jimmy, did Mary write your name in the space for hug? If your name isn't in there, you need to respect her space." Also, there are three blank ovals for students to write their own types of touch. You are encouraged to review these and consult with a counselor if needed.

Grade 3 or 4, continue here: Lesson 6.0, Grade 3–4, #2

"We are now going to do exercises #2 on your 6.0 lesson. Follow along silently as I read the direction to you." Have students write the different type of touches from the list above on the Student Focus Page. When they finish, have them defend their answers especially if the touch they chose is questionable. The truth is, it's hard for schools to regulate what is and isn't appropriate. The reason for this is circumstances. Circumstances can change everything. For example, students kissing each other behind the school wouldn't be appropriate, but a student could make an argument that getting kissed at school would be appropriate if his/her mom did it when dropping them off for school. These types of discussions are valuable and cause deeper thinking.

15. Touch is a great thing. If you feel loved by being close to people (give examples) then your love language is probably Touch.

16. Most who feel loved by touch have no doubt that this is their love language.

17. Everyone has different comfort levels when it comes to touch.

18. We need to respect the rights of others if they don't want to be touched.

19. If people don't respect our space, we need to tell them or draw our personal safety line. *(Remind students how to draw personal safety line.)*

20. Teacher explains to class their personal preference.
    • **Academic Focus Page [Lesson 6.0, Grade 1–2, #1 & #2]**
    • **Academic Focus Page [Lesson 6.0, Grade 3–4, #2]**
    • **Academic Focus Page [Lesson 6.0, Grade 5–6, #3]**

AFP: Lesson 6.0, Grade 1–2, #1 & #2

Name _____ Date _____ **LESSON 6.0**

SAFE TOUCH

○ *Makes me feel loved.*
○ *I like it.*

1. In each of the bubbles there is a type of touch. You can write one name or several names inside a bubble of people who make you feel good or loved with that type of touch. For example, you could write dad, mom, brother, sister, friend, or anyone else you can think of.

Hug	Wrestling	Handshake
Kiss	Back Scratch	Tickle
Back Rub	High Five	Pat on the Back
Snuggling	Foot Rub	Fist Bump

2. Can you think of three other touches we didn't name?

( ) ( ) ( )

//

HOME CONNECTION SECTION

Everybody has a different comfort level when it comes to touch. Some people like to be touched and some people don't. Some people only like certain people to touch them. All people have a right to choose who is allowed to enter their personal space. We need to be respectful of a person's personal space even if their love language is Touch.

GRADES 1 & 2

AFP: Lesson 6.0, Grade 3–4, #2

Name _____ Date _____ **LESSON 6.0**

SAFE TOUCH

○ *Makes me feel loved.*
○ *I like it.*

WHO CONNECTS WITH YOU?

1. Draw a line from a type of touch on the left to the people who connect with you using that touch on the right. You may be surprised that some of these are considered touch. It's okay if you don't have a lot of lines; everyone is different.

HINT:
Use a different colored pencil for each box of people.

Hug
Kiss on the cheek
Back rub
Foot rub
Pat on the back
Snuggling
Wrestling
High five
Head rub
Sitting close
Holding hands

| GRANDFATHER GRANDMOTHER |
| BROTHER SISTER |
| DAD MOM |
| AUNT UNCLE |
| OTHER RELATIVE OR FRIEND |

WHAT IS APPROPRIATE?

2. From the list of touches above, write the ones you think would be appropriate at school. If the teacher were to ask you, "Why do you think the touches you chose are appropriate at school?" could you support your answers with evidence that makes sense?

_____
_____

//

HOME CONNECTION SECTION

Everybody has a different comfort level when it comes to touch. Some people like to be touched and some people don't. Some people only like certain people to touch them. All people have a right to choose what their comfort level is. We need to be respectful of a person's personal space, even if their love language is Touch.

GRADES 3 & 4

"We are now going to do exercise #3 on your 6.0 lesson. Follow along silently as I read the directions to you." Have students list as many ways they can think of that would be considered appropriate or safe touch at school. Encourage them to use school rules or policies to build their list. When they are finished, ask students to volunteer answers. Place special emphasis on asking "why" we have a school policy regarding touch.

Obviously the way you use touch at home with your parents is a lot different from when you are at school. I'm going to list some ways you can use touch at school, and I'm going to be asking for some volunteers to come up and show us how they are done. *(List on the board: 1. High Five, 2. Shaking hands, 3. Gently patting each other on the back, 4. Fist bumping, 5. Putting a hand on a shoulder. Have pairs of students come up and demonstrate each of the ways. Have the class describe times/scenarios when it would be appropriate to demonstrate these kinds of touch.)* **Did you notice they weren't shoving their back or grabbing their hand really hard? When we respect each other's personal space, it creates a friendly and comfortable environment. People naturally like touch, and we should be looking for ways to appropriately make them feel loved through touch if it's okay with them. Unfortunately, some people are inappropriate in the way they touch other people, and we need to talk about how this happens. Let's all get serious now and talk about the opposite of safe touch.**

[TRANSITION TO OPPOSITE]

ANTICIPATORY SET:

The opposite of safe touch is unsafe touch. This kind of touch can be very confusing for children. The topic we are now going to discuss is never comfortable, but it's extremely important. By learning about unsafe touch, you may be able to help a lot of people, including yourself. Is everyone ready to be serious? Okay, let's get started.

TEACHING/PRESENTATION:

There are three categories of touch:

(Write these three categories on the board as you say them.)

> **1. Safe Touch**
> **2. Uncomfortable but Necessary Touch**
> **3. Unsafe Touch**

21. Touch at home is a lot different from touch at school.

22. Teacher lists five ways that students can show appropriate touch at school.
    - High five
    - Handshake
    - Gently patting each other on the back
    - Putting fists together
    - Putting hand on shoulder

23. Teacher has students come up and demonstrate each action while describing when an appropriate time would be to put these actions into place. *(Teacher emphasizes the need to be gentle when doing this by giving examples of what the students didn't do, e.g., shoving.)*

24. Respecting the personal space of others creates a friendly and comfortable environment.

25. People naturally like touch. We should be looking for ways to appropriately touch them if it's okay with them.

26. Unfortunately some people aren't appropriate. *(Teacher transitions to unsafe touch by having students get serious.)*

[TRANSITION TO OPPOSITE]

ANTICIPATORY SET:
1. Introduce unsafe touch.
2. Confusing for children
3. Never comfortable to talk about

Name _____ Date _____ **LESSON 6.0**

SAFE TOUCH

○ *Makes me feel loved.*
○ *I like it.*

1. Thinking deeper: We know that babies require touch to be healthy, but why? Write your best prediction for why you believe touch is required for a baby to be healthy. Use scientific examples if you know of any.

2. Thinking about different cultures and different styles: What are some ways that you have observed people greeting each other or celebrating an accomplishment? For example, I've seen people give high fives after they make a goal playing soccer. Now it's your turn:

3. Obviously the way you use touch at home with your family or during sports is a lot different than when you are at school. List as many ways that you can think of that would be appropriate or considered safe touch at school. Your school rules should help you with the answers:

Everybody has a different comfort level when it comes to touch. Some people like to be touched and some people don't. Some people only like certain people to touch them. All people have a right to choose what their comfort level is. We need to be respectful of a person's personal space even if their love language is Touch.

GRADES 5 & 6

Lesson 6.1, Grades 1–6, #1

"We are now going to do exercise #1 on your 6.1 lesson. Follow along silently as I read the directions to you." Have students copy the three items you wrote on the board and fill in the blanks for A, B, and C.

First, there's safe touch, and we have already talked a lot about that. Safe touch is touch that people need to be healthy. *(Display a picture of a baby, if you have one.)* **When we are babies we need a lot of touch so we can feel safe and relaxed. Safe touch is always appropriate and makes us feel loved. But we haven't talked about the other two categories yet. The second category of touch is called "uncomfortable but necessary touch."**

Uncomfortable but necessary touch can also be considered safe touch. Most of us might not think of it as safe touch, but it is. It's safe touch because it keeps us healthy. *(Show the picture of a doctor helping a child or just a picture of a doctor if you have it.)* **Uncomfortable but necessary touch is what doctors have to do sometimes. When we go in for a physical or a checkup, sometimes they have to check our whole body, including parts that others don't usually see, let alone touch. I'm telling you about this because if you haven't already gone to the doctor for a physical, you might be surprised when they do this. If you have already been to the doctor and they checked your private parts, then you know what I'm talking about when I say, "Uncomfortable but necessary." Yes, it's uncomfortable, but it's really important that a health professional do that to make sure you are completely healthy. Also, sometimes parents have to check their children for health reasons or they may need to bathe them. Really little kids don't usually wash themselves, and I've never seen a baby jump into the bathtub and take a bath. They need their parents' help and supervision. So uncomfortable but necessary touch is safe, but it's definitely uncomfortable. This leads us to the third category, which is "inappropriate or unsafe touch."**

Inappropriate or unsafe touch can leave children feeling confused, hurt, angry, guilty, sad, or scared. When somebody touches somebody else inappropriately, it doesn't make them feel loved. *(Show a picture of a boy and girl in swimsuits if you have one.)* **For this lesson, inappropriate or unsafe touch is being touched by someone where the swimsuit covers. Now some of you in here may be thinking, "Why is (he/she) talking to us about this?" I'm glad if you are thinking that because it tells me that nobody has probably ever touched you inappropriately. We still need to have this discussion, however, because it does happen to a few children, and it could happen to you. I want you to be trained on how to deal with it if it happens to you or a friend. Is everyone following me so far?** *(Rhetorical)* **Okay.**

Most of you have been trained to stay away from strangers. Help me finish this

4. Learning this can help a lot of people.

5. Time to get serious

TEACHING/PRESENTATION:

1. Three categories of touch:
   (Write these on the board.)
   - Safe Touch
   - Uncomfortable but Necessary Touch
   - Inappropriate or Unsafe Touch

2. **Academic Focus Page**
   [Lesson 6.1, Grade 1– 6, #1]

3. Good Touch we have already talked about. *(Give brief examples and put picture of baby up.)*

4. Uncomfortable but necessary touch . . . is a good touch even though it may not seem like it. *(Put doctor picture up.)*

5. Give examples of medical physical/doctor checkup.

6. It's really important for them to check your body to make sure you are healthy.

7. Parents have to check kids for health reasons and bathe them.

8. Inappropriate or unsafe touch leaves kids feeling confused, hurt, angry, guilty, sad, or scared, and it never makes them feel loved. *(Place picture of children in swimsuits up.)*

9. Inappropriate or unsafe touch is being touched in areas that the swimsuit covers.

10. Some of you may be thinking, "Why am I talking about this?" I'm glad if you are because that means you probably haven't been touched inappropriately.

AFP: Lesson 6.1, Grade 1–2, #1

Name _____ Date _____

LESSON 6.1
HOME CONNECTION SECTION

TOUCH (PERSONAL SAFETY)

1. What are the three types of touch? (Hint: one of them is a "not safe" behavior)

   A. _____
   B. _____
   C. _____

2. If **unsafe** touch is going to happen to a child, it's usually done by someone they:

   A. _____
   B. _____
   C. _____

3. What are some reasons a child may not tell someone if a person they know, trust, or love touches them in an **unsafe** way?

   A. _____ B. _____

AFP: Lesson 6.1, Grade 3–4, #1

Name _____ Date _____

LESSON 6.1
HOME CONNECTION SECTION

TOUCH (PERSONAL SAFETY)

1. What are the three types of touch? (Hint: one of them is a "not safe" behavior)

   A. _____
   B. _____
   C. _____

2. If **unsafe** touch is going to happen to a child, it's usually done by someone they:

   A. _____
   B. _____
   C. _____

3. What are some reasons a child may not tell someone if a person they know, trust, or love touches them in an **unsafe** way?

   A. _____ B. _____

AFP: Lesson 6.1, Grade 5–6, #1

Name _____ Date _____

LESSON 6.1
HOME CONNECTION SECTION

TOUCH (PERSONAL SAFETY)

1. What are the three types of touch? (Hint: one of them is a "not safe" behavior)

   A. _____
   B. _____
   C. _____

2. If **unsafe** touch is going to happen to a child, it's usually done by someone they:

   A. _____
   B. _____
   C. _____

3. What are some reasons a child may not tell someone if a person they know, trust, or love touches them in an **unsafe** way?

   A. _____ B. _____
   C. _____ D. _____
   E. _____ F. _____

4. Who is the first person most kids tell when something bad happens to them?

   _____ but they should tell _____

5. If someone touches you or a friend in an **unsafe way**, you always need to tell at least two adults:

   A. An adult who lives in your _____ .
   B. And an adult who works at _____ .

Here are some good tips to be safe:
   - Avoid situations where you might have to be alone with someone that you feel uneasy about. Tell your parents privately that you don't want to be with them.
   - Follow your instincts. If it doesn't seem right then don't do it.
   - If someone is bothering you, tell them to "Stop!" and draw your personal safety line.
   - If you aren't sure about someone's behavior, ask your parents or an adult at school.

And remember, it's not likely to happen to you, so don't be afraid of everybody and everything. These lessons are to teach you how to be wise and safe!

GRADES 5 & 6

sentence: "Never talk to . . ." *(strangers).* **Believe me, this is good advice. Kids are usually taught by their parents to stay away from strangers. If you and a friend went to the park and had to use the restroom and you saw some creepy-looking guy standing outside the bathroom door, you would probably say to yourself, "I'm not going in there." You'd use a different bathroom or take an adult with you. Generally, when kids see someone they don't know, their danger and caution feelings go off and they avoid the person. Learning to stay away from strangers keeps you from getting into situations that might be harmful. But I'm going to tell you something that a lot of kids don't know.** *(Lower the volume of your voice for dramatic effect and go on.)* **Most of the unsafe touch that happens to kids doesn't happen by a stranger; it happens by someone they know, trust, or love.**

Grades 1–6, continue here:	Lesson 6.1, Grade 1–6, #2

"We are now going to fill in the blanks for #2 on your 6.1 lesson. Follow along silently as I read the direction to you." Have students write "know," "trust," "love" in the three spaces provided (A, B, C respectively).

Why do you think this is so? *(Call on students who have their hands raised. Help guide them in the discussion toward the main point, which is "because they need to get close to you so they can do that.")* **Right, they need to get close to you. If a stranger tried to touch you in an unsafe way, you would probably run away or scream. At least I hope you would. But people who touch kids inappropriately have to get close to them, gain their trust, and maybe even try to convince them that what they are doing is okay. This puts kids in a really bad position. Think about it: If someone you know, trust, or love inappropriately touched you or tried to touch you, it would be really confusing, wouldn't it?** *(Rhetorical)* **I mean, here is someone you know, trust, or love, and now they are doing something to you that you know isn't right. Why do you think this would be so confusing?** *(Because you trust them, and now you don't know what to do.)* **Yes, it's really confusing because you know they shouldn't have done that but you don't know what to do because you thought they were someone you could trust. I mean it could be a friend of the family, neighbor, babysitter, or relative. So my next question to you is, "What would you do if this did happen?"** *(Students will typically say, "Tell my parents, or tell someone.")* **Sure, telling your parents would be a good idea, and I definitely agree that you should tell someone. Why do you think some kids might not tell anybody?** *(Because they love them, they are a friend, they don't want them to get in trouble, they could be embarrassed, they think people might not believe them, or someone threatened them. Make sure all of these answers are brought up and every student understands this concept. This is one of the most critical points for students to understand. Write them on the board.)*

11. We need to talk about this:
    - it could happen to you
    - it could happen to your friend

12. Most of you have been trained to stay away from strangers. *(Have students finish sentence. Never talk to . . . (strangers).*

13. Teacher tells story about kids avoiding bathroom if there was a creepy guy standing outside.

14. Staying away from strangers is good, but unfortunately most inappropriate or unsafe touch happens by people we know, trust, and love. (Say: "Why do you think this is so?" They need to get close to you so they can do that.)
    - **Academic Focus Page [Lesson 6.1, Grade 1–6, #2]**

15. People we know, trust, and love are able to get close to us and maybe even try to convince us that what they are doing is okay.

16. Kids who are inappropriately touched by someone they know, trust, or love are placed in a really confusing situation.

17. (Say: "Why do you think this would be confusing?" Because you know them, and now you don't know what to do.)

18. (Ask: "What would you do if this did happen?")

19. (Ask: "Why do you think some students might not tell?" List these examples on board as they are named. Every student needs to understand these six.)
    - They love them.
    - They are a friend.

AFP: Lesson 6.1, Grade 1–2, #2

Name _____ Date _____

LESSON 6.1
HOME CONNECTION SECTION

TOUCH (PERSONAL SAFETY)

1. What are the three types of touch? (Hint: one of them is a "not safe" behavior)

   A. _____

   B. _____

   C. _____

2. If **unsafe** touch is going to happen to a child, it's usually done by someone they:

   A. _____

   B. _____

   C. _____

3. What are some reasons a child may not tell someone if a person they know, trust, or love touches them in an **unsafe** way?

   A. _____ B. _____

AFP: Lesson 6.1, Grade 3–4, #2

Name _____ Date _____

LESSON 6.1
HOME CONNECTION SECTION

TOUCH (PERSONAL SAFETY)

1. What are the three types of touch? (Hint: one of them is a "not safe" behavior)

   A. _____

   B. _____

   C. _____

2. If **unsafe** touch is going to happen to a child, it's usually done by someone they:

   A. _____

   B. _____

   C. _____

3. What are some reasons a child may not tell someone if a person they know, trust, or love touches them in an **unsafe** way?

   A. _____ B. _____

AFP: Lesson 6.1, Grade 5–6, #2

Name _____ Date _____

LESSON 6.1
HOME CONNECTION SECTION

TOUCH (PERSONAL SAFETY)

1. What are the three types of touch? (Hint: one of them is a "not safe" behavior)

   A. _____

   B. _____

   C. _____

2. If **unsafe** touch is going to happen to a child, it's usually done by someone they:

   A. _____

   B. _____

   C. _____

3. What are some reasons a child may not tell someone if a person they know, trust, or love touches them in an **unsafe** way?

   A. _____ B. _____

   C. _____ D. _____

   E. _____ F. _____

4. Who is the first person most kids tell when something bad happens to them?

   _____ but they should tell _____

5. If someone touches you or a friend in an **unsafe way**, you always need to tell at least two adults:

   A. An adult who lives in your _____.

   B. And an adult who works at _____.

Here are some good tips to be safe:
- Avoid situations where you might have to be alone with someone that you feel uneasy about. Tell your parents privately that you don't want to be with them.
- Follow your instincts. If it doesn't seem right then don't do it.
- If someone is bothering you, tell them to "Stop!" and draw your personal safety line.
- If you aren't sure about someone's behavior, ask your parents or an adult at school.

And remember, it's not likely to happen to you, so don't be afraid of everybody and everything. These lessons are to teach you how to be wise and safe!

GRADES 5 & 6

Grades 1–6, continue here: Lesson 6.1, Grades 1–6, #3

"We are now going to fill in the blanks for #3 on your 6.1 lesson. Follow along silently as I read the direction to you." Have students write the six reasons why in the spaces provided (these should be written on your white board). A. They love them, B. They are a friend, C. Don't want them to get in trouble, D. They are embarrassed, E. People might not believe them, F. Someone threatened them.

And if a student does tell someone what happened, who do you think they tell first? *(Students will usually say parents, teacher, etc., but when they do I always respond with, "I wish that were true." If someone doesn't come up with "their friend," then give them the correct answer.)* **When bad things happen to kids, they usually tell their best friends, but they should tell a parent or trusted adult.**

Grades 1–6, continue here: Lesson 6.1, Grades 1–6, #4

"We are now going to fill in the blanks for #4 on your 6.1 lesson. Follow along silently as I read the direction to you." Have students fill in the blanks with "best friend" and "trusted adult."

Unfortunately, they usually tell someone a long time after it happens to them. Sometimes it can be years later! Let me tell you why this is so bad. It's bad because even though not very many people do these things to kids, the ones who do tend to affect a lot of kids. They rarely inappropriately touch just one kid. If a kid takes a long time to tell someone what happened to them, then the person who did it may be out there affecting other kids' lives. Can you see why it's so important to tell someone if it happens to you? *(Rhetorical)* **And now can you see why this training is really important?** *(Rhetorical)* **Even though no one may do something to you, they might do it to your friend, and this means that it's your responsibility to help. Now, let's talk about what we want you to do if something happens to you or your friend.**

1. **We want you to tell your parents or trusted adult if you are able.**
2. **We want you to tell an adult at school. This can be any adult who works at school like your teacher, a past teacher, counselor, school nurse, principal, or secretary.**
3. **If your friend tells you that something happened to them, tell your parents and an adult at school.**

The first thing to do is tell your parents or trusted adult when you get a chance.

- They don't want them to get into trouble.
- They are embarrassed.
- They think people might not believe them.
- Someone has threatened them.

20. **Academic Focus Page [Lesson 6.1, Grade 1–6, #3]**

21. (Ask: "If a kid does tell someone, who do you think they tell first? Use the "I wish that were true" responses. Make sure they come up with "Their friend.")

- **Academic Focus Page [Lesson 6.1, Grade 1–6, #4]**

22. When bad things happen to kids they usually tell their best friend.

23. This is bad because they usually tell them a long time after it happens.

24. This is bad because one person can affect a lot of kids during the time it takes for them to tell.

25. See why it's really important to tell someone?

26. If this happens to you or a friend we want you to:
- tell your parents or a trusted adult if you are able.
- tell any adult who works at school. *(Give examples.)*

27. If it happens to your friend tell both your parents and a trusted adult at school.

28. If it happens to you, tell your parents or trusted adult.

29. Be safely away from the person who did it.

30. If they tell you not to tell, say, "Okay," and do your best acting job.

AFP: Lesson 6.1, Grade 1–2, #3 & #4

Name _____ Date _____

LESSON 6.1
HOME CONNECTION SECTION

TOUCH (PERSONAL SAFETY)

1. What are the three types of touch? (Hint: one of them is a "not safe" behavior)
   A. _____
   B. _____
   C. _____

2. If **unsafe** touch is going to happen to a child, it's usually done by someone they:
   A. _____
   B. _____
   C. _____

3. What are some reasons a child may not tell someone if a person they know, trust, or love touches them in an **unsafe** way?
   A. _____   B. _____

AFP: Lesson 6.1, Grade 3–4, #3 & #4

Name _____ Date _____

LESSON 6.1
HOME CONNECTION SECTION

TOUCH (PERSONAL SAFETY)

1. What are the three types of touch? (Hint: one of them is a "not safe" behavior)
   A. _____
   B. _____
   C. _____

2. If **unsafe** touch is going to happen to a child, it's usually done by someone they:
   A. _____
   B. _____
   C. _____

3. What are some reasons a child may not tell someone if a person they know, trust, or love touches them in an **unsafe** way?
   A. _____   B. _____

AFP: Lesson 6.1, Grade 5–6, #3 & #4

Name _____ Date _____

LESSON 6.1
HOME CONNECTION SECTION

TOUCH (PERSONAL SAFETY)

1. What are the three types of touch? (Hint: one of them is a "not safe" behavior)
   A. _____
   B. _____
   C. _____

2. If **unsafe** touch is going to happen to a child, it's usually done by someone they:
   A. _____
   B. _____
   C. _____

3. What are some reasons a child may not tell someone if a person they know, trust, or love touches them in an **unsafe** way?
   A. _____   B. _____
   C. _____   D. _____
   E. _____   F. _____

4. Who is the first person most kids tell when something bad happens to them?
   _____ but they should tell _____

5. If someone touches you or a friend in an **unsafe way**, you always need to tell at least two adults:
   A. An adult who lives in your _____.
   B. And an adult who works at _____.

Here are some good tips to be safe:
- Avoid situations where you might have to be alone with someone that you feel uneasy about. Tell your parents privately that you don't want to be with them.
- Follow your instincts. If it doesn't seem right then don't do it.
- If someone is bothering you, tell them to "Stop!" and draw your personal safety line.
- If you aren't sure about someone's behavior, ask your parents or an adult at school.

And remember, it's not likely to happen to you, so don't be afraid of everybody and everything. These lessons are to teach you how to be wise and safe!

GRADES 5 & 6

Make sure you are safe and not near the person who did it to you. They may freak out if they know you are going to tell someone. If the person who did something to you says, "Don't tell anyone," do your best acting job and say, "I won't." Try not to be upset, and when you can, go and tell someone. Remember when we talked about bribery last time? *(Rhetorical)* People who give you gifts to get something? *(Rhetorical)* If someone does something to you and then gives you a gift not to tell, take the gift, act happy, and go tell someone the first chance you get. Think about this: if you look really upset or turn down their gift, they may get scared because they know you are going to tell someone. If they get scared, they might try to keep you from telling. So no matter what, do your best acting job and make them feel like everything is fine, then go and tell someone when you are safe. Any questions about that? *(Answer questions)*

The second thing to do is tell a trusted adult at school no matter what. Even if your parents tell you they will take care of it, we still want you to tell an adult at school. Sometimes parents are put in a weird position and may not want to tell anyone for the same reasons that kids sometimes don't want to tell anyone. If you tell an adult at school, we have to do something about it. We are called "mandatory reporters," and it's against the law for us not to help you. Always tell an adult at school. Any questions about that?

Third, if a friend tells you that something bad happened to them, we want you to tell your parents if you can and an adult at school. If your friend begs you not to tell, we still need you to tell someone. Remember, every day you wait to tell an adult, the person who did that to your friend could be out there doing it to some other kid. Tell your friend you care about them and that this is one secret you can't keep. Offer to go with them to tell an adult at school. If they won't go with you, go by yourself. No matter what, tell an adult who works at school. You could be helping a lot of other kids.

Grades 1–6, continue here:	Lesson 6.1, Grade 1–6, #5

"We are now going to fill in the blanks for #5 on your 6.1 lesson. Follow along silently as I read the direction to you." Have students write "home" and "school."

Here are some good tips to keep you safe:

1. Avoid situations where you might have to be alone with someone you feel uneasy about. If you don't want to be alone with someone tell your parents privately.
2. Follow your instincts. If something doesn't seem right, then don't do it.
3. If someone is bothering you, tell them to stop, draw your personal safety line, and get away.

31. If they offer you a bribe/gift after they've done an unsafe touch *(explain bribe again)*, take it and do your best acting job.

32. Don't give them a reason to keep you from leaving.

33. (Ask students if they need clarification.)

34. Tell a trusted adult at school no matter what, even if parents say they will take care of it. We always want you to tell an adult who works at school. We are mandatory reporters.

35. (Ask students if they need clarification.)

36. If a friend tells you that it happened to them, tell your parents and a trusted adult at school.

37. Even if your friend begs you not to tell, you need to tell an adult at school.

38. Offer to go with them to tell an adult at school.

39. Go by yourself if they won't go with you.

40. You could be protecting a lot of other children.

    • **Academic Focus Page [Lesson 6.1, Grade 1–6, #5]**

41. Here are some good tips to be safe:
    • Avoid situations where you might have to be alone with someone you feel uneasy about. Tell your parents privately that you don't want to be with them.
    • Follow your instincts. If it doesn't seem right then don't do it.

AFP: Lesson 6.1, Grade 1–2, #5

Name _____ Date _____

LESSON 6.1
HOME CONNECTION SECTION

TOUCH (PERSONAL SAFETY)

1. What are the three types of touch? (Hint: one of them is a "not safe" behavior)
   A. _____
   B. _____
   C. _____

2. If **unsafe** touch is going to happen to a child, it's usually done by someone they:
   A. _____
   B. _____
   C. _____

3. What are some reasons a child may not tell someone if a person they know, trust, or love touches them in an **unsafe** way?
   A. _____ B. _____

AFP: Lesson 6.1, Grade 3–4, #5

Name _____ Date _____

LESSON 6.1
HOME CONNECTION SECTION

TOUCH (PERSONAL SAFETY)

1. What are the three types of touch? (Hint: one of them is a "not safe" behavior)
   A. _____
   B. _____
   C. _____

2. If **unsafe** touch is going to happen to a child, it's usually done by someone they:
   A. _____
   B. _____
   C. _____

3. What are some reasons a child may not tell someone if a person they know, trust, or love touches them in an **unsafe** way?
   A. _____ B. _____

AFP: Lesson 6.1, Grade 5–6, #5

Name _____ Date _____

LESSON 6.1
HOME CONNECTION SECTION

TOUCH (PERSONAL SAFETY)

1. What are the three types of touch? (Hint: one of them is a "not safe" behavior)
   A. _____
   B. _____
   C. _____

2. If **unsafe** touch is going to happen to a child, it's usually done by someone they:
   A. _____
   B. _____
   C. _____

3. What are some reasons a child may not tell someone if a person they know, trust, or love touches them in an **unsafe** way?
   A. _____ B. _____
   C. _____ D. _____
   E. _____ F. _____

4. Who is the first person most kids tell when something bad happens to them?
   _____ but they should tell _____

5. If someone touches you or a friend in an **unsafe way**, you always need to tell at least two adults:
   A. An adult who lives in your _____.
   B. And an adult who works at _____.

Here are some good tips to be safe:
   • Avoid situations where you might have to be alone with someone that you feel uneasy about. Tell your parents privately that you don't want to be with them.
   • Follow your instincts. If it doesn't seem right then don't do it.
   • If someone is bothering you, tell them to "Stop!" and draw your personal safety line.
   • If you aren't sure about someone's behavior, ask your parents or an adult at school.

And remember, it's not likely to happen to you, so don't be afraid of everybody and everything. These lessons are to teach you how to be wise and safe!

GRADES 5 & 6

LESSON

6

ABBREVIATED

Safe Touch

145

4. If you aren't sure about someone's behavior, ask your parents or talk to an adult at school. Let them know if someone is acting weird or doing weird things around you. Get their advice.

We talked about why kids don't tell adults what happened to them. One thing I mentioned is that it would be embarrassing. Let's face it: it's not exactly the easiest thing to say, "He touched me there." But what I want you to know is that I won't go into shock if you tell me. *[I usually act dramatic and say, "Oh no, I can't believe this happened," and I act shocked. Then I stop and say, "I'm not going to do that if you tell me. I'm going to calmly ask you to tell me a little bit about what happened, and then we will go from there. There's virtually nothing you can tell me that would send me into shock. I've heard it all. I know it's not the easiest conversation to have, but it's really important. Bring a friend with you if you want. We will work on your problem together."]*

Finally, I want you to know it is very unlikely that any of this will ever happen to you. I don't want you to be suspicious or scared of people, thinking, "What if it's this person or that person?" Those kinds of thoughts won't get you anywhere. Remember that most people would never dream of doing anything bad to children. I want you to be informed and safe and know what to do if it happens to you or a friend. That's all.

Now I want everybody to take a deep breath and hold it. *(After a heavy discussion with students, I usually always have them do a breathing exercise. When I'm teaching this subject, I can usually feel the tension in the room.)* Let it out. Take another deep breath and hold it. Let it out. Let's talk about the positive side of touch. It's a lot more fun.

CLOSURE:

Today we talked about the love language called Touch. Some people feel really loved when they are hugged, kissed, or in physical contact with other people. If touch makes you feel loved, then it's probably your love language.

We found out that whether your love language is Touch or not, we still need to respect the rights of others who don't want to be touched. They may like touch, but not from you. This is okay, because we need to honor their personal space.

If we don't want other people to touch us, it's important for us to communicate this. They may not realize we don't like it. If they keep bothering us with touch, we should draw our personal safety line and tell someone.

We learned that appropriate touch at school can include high fives, shaking hands, fist-bumping, patting someone on the back gently, or putting a hand on their shoulder.

We also learned there are two other types of touch, uncomfortable but necessary touch and inappropriate or unsafe touch.

- If someone is bothering you, tell them to "stop" and draw your personal safety line.
- If you aren't sure about someone's behavior, ask your parents or an adult at school. Let them know if someone is acting weird or doing weird things around you. Get their advice.

42. We talked about the reasons kids don't tell anyone. I mentioned that embarrassment is one of those reasons. It's never comfortable to tell someone what happened. The person who did that to you is counting on you being too embarrassed to tell. Trust me: If you tell me, I won't go into shock. *(Teacher does a dramatic shock appearance, and then calmly tells class how they will really handle it.)* I will help you solve your problem. Bring a friend with you if you want.

43. It is unlikely that this will ever happen to you. Most people will not harm you. I don't want you to be scared and suspicious. I want you to be informed and safe and know what to do if this happens to you or a friend. That's all.

44. *(Everybody take a breath exercise.)* Transition to closure and assignment.

CLOSURE:

Today we talked about the love language called Touch. Some people feel really loved when they are hugged, kissed, or in physical contact with other people. If touch makes you feel loved, then it's probably your love language.

We found out that whether your love language is Touch or not we still need to respect the rights of others who don't want to be touched. They may like touch, but not from us. This is okay, and we should honor their personal space.

If we don't want other people to touch us, it's important for us to communicate this. They may not realize we don't like it. If they keep bothering us with touch, we can draw our personal safety line and tell someone.

We learned that appropriate touch at school can include, high fives, shaking hands, fist bumping, patting someone on the back gently, or putting a hand on their shoulder.

We also learned that there are two other types of touch, uncomfortable but necessary touch, and inappropriate or unsafe touch.

Uncomfortable touch is when a doctor has to check our bodies for health reasons, which can include touching our private parts. This may not always seem like a safe touch, but it is.

Inappropriate or unsafe touch is when someone touches our body in places where a swimsuit normally covers. If this happens to us we need to:

1. Tell our parents if we can.
2. Always tell an adult who works at your school.
3. If our friend tells us that it happened to them, we need to tell our parents and an adult who works at our school, even if our friend begs us not too.

Finally we learned that it is unlikely a student will have to deal with inappropriate or unsafe touch. Most adults would never think about doing something bad to children. We don't have to be suspicious or scared of people. Learning about inappropriate or unsafe touch is just one more way for us to know what to do if it does happen, and one more way to be safe. Knowing what to do might help a lot of other children.

I would like you to think about what you were taught today and ask yourself, "Do I just like touch, or does it make me feel loved?" Please fill in a circle by one of the items at the top right-hand side of your Academic Focus Page. The items say, "Makes me feel loved," or "I like it." This is the last of the 5 Love Languages. Remember, the five are: Words of Affirmation, Quality Time, Acts of Service, Gifts, and Touch. For next time, I want you to choose your two favorites. I hope you can figure out which one you like the best and which one is your second favorite.

INDEPENDENT PRACTICE/ASSIGNMENT:

Have each student do the following:

1. Suggest that each student give their parents a hug (don't make this mandatory). Tell students that if they have never given their parent a hug or haven't hugged them in a long time, they should give it a try and see what happens.
2. Tell the students to think about the 5 Love Languages and choose two of them. Have them think about which is their favorite, and which is their second favorite. Let them know you will be asking which languages they chose the next time you teach the lesson.
3. Tell the students when you will return to teach the next lesson. Remind them that you will be asking various students about their experience the next time you teach the love languages.
4. Review the objectives set on the white board. Have students tell a neighbor what they learned and what they would do. Ask if there are any questions and clarify misunderstandings.

Uncomfortable touch is when a doctor has to check our bodies for health reasons, which can include our private parts. This may not always seem like a safe touch, but it is.

Inappropriate or unsafe touch is when someone touches our body in places where a swimsuit normally covers. If this happens to us we need to:

1. Tell our parents if we can.
2. Always tell an adult who works at school.
3. If our friend tells us it happened to them, we need to tell our parents and an adult who works at school, even if our friend begs us not too.

Finally we learned that it is unlikely that a student will have to deal with unsafe touch. Most adults would never think about doing something bad to children. We don't have to be suspicious or scared of people. Learning about unsafe touch is just one more way for us to know what to do if it does happen, and one more way to be safe. Knowing what to do might help a lot of other children.

Think about what you were taught today and ask yourself, "Do I just like touch, or does it make me feel loved?" Please fill in a circle by one of the items at the top right-hand side of your Academic Focus Page. The items say, "Makes me feel loved," or "I like it." This is the last of the five love languages. Remember, the five are: Words of Affirmation, Quality Time, Acts of Service, Gifts, and Touch. Choose your two favorites for next time. Hopefully you can figure which one you like the best and which one is your second favorite.

INDEPENDENT PRACTICE/ASSIGNMENT:

Have each student do the following:

1. Suggest that each student give their parents a hug (don't make this mandatory). Tell students that if they have never given their parent a hug or haven't hugged them in a long time, they should give it a try and see what happens.
2. Tell the students to think about the five love languages and choose two of them. Have them think about which is their favorite and which is their second favorite. Let them know you will be asking which languages they chose the next time you teach the lesson.
3. Tell the students when you will return to teach the next lesson. Remind them that you will be asking various students about their experience the next time you teach the love languages.
4. Review the objectives set on the white board. Have students tell a neighbor what they learned and what they would do. Ask if there are any questions and clarify misunderstandings.

FINAL THOUGHTS

When teaching this love language, communicate with your students' parents ahead of time to let them know the nature of this lesson. I had one parent opt their child out of the second half of the lesson because their child had been severely abused. Keep in mind that there may be some of these students in your class, and parents should have the right to opt their child out.

You may be wondering why I use the term "unsafe touch" instead of "bad touch." Many of us learned curriculums that used the terms Good Touch/Bad Touch, but the problem with this is that not all "bad touch" hurts or is unpleasant. This can create confusion with children when we call it "bad touch" but it doesn't seem to be bad to them. Keep in mind that many children have been groomed to believe that what they are experiencing is good or pleasant. They don't have the foresight to realize the long-term damage that can be caused by it. The terminology "unsafe touch" is more accurate because it indicates that the act causes damage and may lead to even worse problems.

Whenever I teach a lesson on child abuse I have another adult present with me. First of all, it documents what I said and how I responded to students who had questions. Second, it allows me to have another set of eyes in the room to observe students for negative body language while I'm teaching. There have been a few times when we have noticed a child acting odd and later discovered that they were involved in some type of abuse. Negative body language can include not making eye contact, wanting to leave the room, and looking pale, nervous, or panic-stricken. Remember, students may simply be uncomfortable with the topic and are exhibiting discomfort. Use discretion when investigating your observations.

Create an approachable atmosphere by being animated. Students love it when teachers act out certain scenarios and make silly faces. Keep a balance between light and serious. The students will be serious when you want them to be. The light side of things makes you appear approachable, and students will feel that it's safe to confide in you.

If children never disclose anything to you, don't feel as if you have failed. A really good friend of mine is a detective who investigates crimes against children. He told me once that most kids don't come forward until they are older. You may be planting the seeds so that someday when a child feels strong enough they can come forward and tell somebody what has happened.

Remember, you are training students to help other students. Small children will usually tell their parents when something bad has happened to them. Teenagers, on the other hand, will usually tell their friends about things that happened to them in the past or present. If children are disclosing abuse when they get older, guess who they tell first? Right, their best friend! While we can't put an exact number on how many abuse cases there are each year, we know that a larger percentage of children won't be abused. When you are teaching about abuse, keep this in mind. You are training the larger group to support and identify the less-fortunate smaller group. By training all students to identify child abuse, you are enabling them to seek help faster for their friends. This in itself is an excellent accomplishment.

FROM THE CLASSROOM

I taught this lesson to a third grade class and when I taught the final lesson I went through the usual review, asked students to volunteer any experiences they had, and asked if any of them had figured out if their love language was touch. A girl raised her hand.

"Ashley, what would you like to say?" I said, calling on her.

"Mr. Freed, I know my love language is definitely touch."

"How do you know that?" I said.

"Because whenever we all sit in the living room to watch movies, I'm always the first one to try to sit by my mom or my dad. I really like to snuggle, and it makes me feel loved. And you want to know something else?" she said.

"What's that?" I questioned.

"I really think it's fun when my dad is lying on his back and sleeping and I use his belly as a pillow. I like to listen to him breathe. That really makes me feel loved."

We all laughed with her, and I thought, *Now there's a girl who's figured out her love language.*

CHAPTER 8
Choosing Your Love Languages

INTRODUCTION

Congratulations! You have reached the final lesson. This lesson focuses on putting into action all you have previously taught and brings your students to a decision-making point. They will be deciding what their primary and secondary love languages are. This is always an exciting day because it gives students an opportunity not only to pick their love languages, but to see how they match up with others in the classroom. You will gain a lot of insight and understanding about each other.

This lesson starts off with a recap of the five love languages and gives some practical examples of what each might look like. After this, you will spend some time explaining to the class that picking their favorite love languages is a lot like going to an ice cream shop. Once they get to the shop they don't pick a flavor because it's their friend's favorite; instead they pick their favorite flavor. This explanation is necessary because it helps to limit peer-pressure factors and allows students to pick the languages that make them feel loved.

The actual process where the student indicates to you their love language should be done in such a way that there is little or no bias. This is quickly and easily accomplished by having students put their heads on their desks, raising their hands, and indicating with a number of fingers (1–5) their primary and secondary choices. While their heads are down you can use the form I created or your own class roster to record responses. A key point when recording student information is to make sure the information is easy to understand by others (counselor, secretary, school nurse, or administrator) for later use. It is preferable to have the whole building use the same recording system. For example, I used a number system 1 = Words of Affirmation, 2 = Quality Time, etc. next to each student's name. You want to think about keeping a record of your students' love languages for their teachers next year. This information can be helpful even though they should be teaching the love languages again the following year. Using a SharePoint folder or passing the information along electronically is great as well. The advantage to the new teacher is tremendous because he or she can start building a deeper connection with the students from day one.

Once you have recorded the class's primary and secondary languages it's on to great fun by dividing them up into their primary and secondary groups. I usually point out five locations in the classroom and have the students go to the spot that coordinates with their love language choice. We repeat this process for their secondary choice as well.

Dividing the students into their respective love language groups will give you a good feel for how the class is composed. You will get a visual demonstration of whether the class is dispersed evenly or extremely lopsided. During this time, students will also have the opportunity to visually experience who is in their group. Sometimes seeing other students in their own group can help break down walls of conflict. Students who previously thought they had nothing in common with a fellow student can now see they share the same love language. The love languages have the ability to transcend academic, athletic, popular, cultural, racial, or other differences. This is one of many advantages to teaching the love languages.

When students have had a chance to see each other in their primary and secondary groups, they'll return to their seats and record their own love languages to be a visual reminder for them and for you. Make sure the students record their love languages on some type of placard that can be affixed to their desk in a lasting way. Some teachers prefer to have the students make temporary placards until more permanent ones can be made or laminated. Attaching these placards to their desks will make it easier for you to identify a specific student's love language as you teach throughout the day. Be sure to read the information following this chapter that pertains to your specific discipline and details how to use the love language information.

The culminating activity will involve a classroom discussion. This is where you and your class will sit together and discuss topics such as how they came to know their love languages, how they think it will help them at home and at school, what they learned about their family, friends, and classmates, and how it could be used to benefit their classroom/school. Having this discussion will be very enlightening as you listen to your students retell stories about their adventures with the love languages. Pay special attention when you discuss how the love languages can benefit the class. Students can come up with some great ideas for making the classroom and playground a wonderful environment. You as the instructor should share with them what you learned. This can either be about you or them. Remind students at some point that you hope to continue this for the rest of the school year. This sends a powerful message that you consider the work they have done and these lessons to be meaningful.

LESSON 7
CHOOSING YOUR LOVE LANGUAGES
(SCRIPTED)

OBJECTIVE:

Students will choose their primary and secondary love languages. The teacher will record the student choices on a form. The students will record their own love language on a placard to be attached to their desk. Students will tell the teacher about what they have learned and how they plan to use this information. Students will formulate a plan to be used in the classroom.

Write on white board:

1. I can describe my top two love languages.
2. I can describe each love language and can use techniques to love people when I know their language.

(Have students talk with each other for thirty seconds about what they think they are going to be learning today.)

REVIEW:

Instructor will ask volunteer students to explain:

1. What is the fifth love language? *(Touch)*
2. Review the last lesson's objective that you wrote on the white board.
3. Call on a few volunteer students to quickly discuss how their assignment went and what they experienced.
4. Call on students to name one of the five love languages until all five are named.

ANTICIPATORY SET:

Today is the big day! All of you will get a chance to pick your top two love languages. These top two languages are called your primary and secondary love languages and will be your first and second choices. Your first choice will be the love language that makes you feel the most loved, and your second choice is the one that makes you feel loved but not quite as much as the first one. Everybody ready? *(Rhetorical)* **Okay, let's get started by taking a simple assessment. This assessment may help you as you decide today.**

LESSON 7

CHOOSING YOUR LOVE LANGUAGES

(ABBREVIATED)

OBJECTIVE:

Students will choose their primary and secondary love languages. The teacher will record the student choices on a form. The students will record their own love language on a placard to be attached to their desk. Students will tell the teacher about what they have learned and how they plan to use this information. Students will formulate a plan to be used in the classroom.

Write on white board:

1. I can describe my top two love languages.
2. I can describe each love language and can use techniques to love people when I know their languages.

(Have students talk with each other for thirty seconds about what they think they are going to be learning today.)

REVIEW:

Instructor will ask volunteer students to explain:

1. What is the fifth love language? *(Touch)*
2. Review the last lesson's objective that you wrote on the white board.
3. Call on a few volunteer students to quickly discuss how their assignment went and what they experienced.
4. Call on students to name one of the five love languages until all five are named.

ANTICIPATORY SET:

1. Everyone gets a chance to pick their top two love languages.

2. First choice is called primary and second choice secondary.

"**Look at the Assessment Page, Lesson 7.0. Read the direction silently as I read it aloud. I'm going to read the list on the left-hand side one at a time. When I read something that makes you feel loved, circle the x in that row. Please don't go ahead. We will do one at a time and then move to the next one.** *(You can let older students do this assessment on their own. This has been written for all grade levels.)* **When we get to the bottom of the page I want you to count the x's in each column and put the number of x's you circled in the space provided. Four x's is the maximum number you can get in any column. Look for the two columns with the most x's. If you have a tie, that's okay. You will have to decide in a moment by making your best guess.** *(Put these aside for now, and we will come back to them in a moment.)*

TEACHING/PRESENTATION:

The first thing we need to do is write the five love languages on the board in the order that they were taught. *(Call on various students and make sure the love languages are written on the board in the order that they were taught. Place a number by each love language, e.g., 1. Words of Affirmation. This will keep things consistent for everyone in the school.)* **Each week we have learned one of these five love languages, and today it is your turn to pick the two that make you feel the most loved—not the two that make your best friend or buddy feel loved, but the two that make you feel the most loved. It's like going to an ice cream shop. If you were standing in front of a whole bunch of different flavors of ice cream and you needed to pick two flavors for your ice cream cone, you wouldn't pick licorice and strawberry because they were your friend's favorite. You would pick the two you really liked. This is how I want you to pick your top two love languages. I want you to choose your top two love languages because they make you feel the most loved. You should be proud of your love languages and not care at all if you are the only one in the room who has that love language. Does everyone understand?** *[This is an important clarifying question because you may have some students who can't decide or like both equally, etc. The answer to any question like this is, "Just pick two you really like even if you're not sure." Once in a while I will have a student who just can't decide between the two, I tell them this is okay and encourage them that maybe someday they will be able to. I still make them pick their primary and secondary by guessing. In my history of teaching the love languages I have only had one student refuse to pick any because he couldn't decide. Rather than ruin his day and mine, I let him sit out. For the normal fence-sitters, I simply nudge them with "Make your best guess."]* **Another thing I want you to understand is this: By choosing your love languages, you will**

3. First choice is the one that makes you feel most loved. Second choice, similar but not quite as much as first choice.

Grades 1–6, continue here: Lesson 7.0, Grade 1–6, Whole Page

"Look at the Assessment Page, Lesson 7.0. Read the direction silently as I read it aloud. I'm going to read the list on the left-hand side one at a time. When I read something that makes you feel loved, circle the x in that row. Please don't go ahead; we will do one at a time and then move to the next one. *(You can let older students do this assessment on their own. This has been written for all grade levels.)* When we get to the bottom of the page, I want you to count the x's in each column and put the number of x's you circled in the space provided. Four x's is the maximum number you can get in any column. Look for the two columns with the most x's. If you have a tie, that's okay. You will have to decide in a moment by making your best guess. *(Put these aside for now and we will come back to them in a moment.)*

AFP: Lesson 7.0, Grade 1–6, Bottom of Page

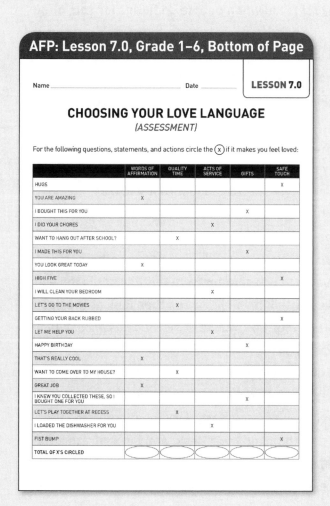

Name _____ Date _____ **LESSON 7.0**

CHOOSING YOUR LOVE LANGUAGE
(ASSESSMENT)

For the following questions, statements, and actions circle the ⊗ if it makes you feel loved:

	WORDS OF AFFIRMATION	QUALITY TIME	ACTS OF SERVICE	GIFTS	SAFE TOUCH
HUGS					X
YOU ARE AMAZING	X				
I BOUGHT THIS FOR YOU				X	
I DID YOUR CHORES			X		
WANT TO HANG OUT AFTER SCHOOL?		X			
I MADE THIS FOR YOU				X	
YOU LOOK GREAT TODAY	X				
HIGH FIVE					X
I WILL CLEAN YOUR BEDROOM			X		
LET'S GO TO THE MOVIES		X			
GETTING YOUR BACK RUBBED					X
LET ME HELP YOU			X		
HAPPY BIRTHDAY				X	
THAT'S REALLY COOL	X				
WANT TO COME OVER TO MY HOUSE?		X			
GREAT JOB	X				
I KNEW YOU COLLECTED THESE, SO I BOUGHT ONE FOR YOU				X	
LET'S PLAY TOGETHER AT RECESS		X			
I LOADED THE DISHWASHER FOR YOU			X		
FIST BUMP					X
TOTAL OF X'S CIRCLED	⬭	⬭	⬭	⬭	⬭

not necessarily be getting more of whatever you choose in here. In other words, don't just choose gifts as your love language because you think I'll give you more gifts than I give to anyone else. It's really important that you pick the two languages that honestly make you feel the most loved. Does everyone understand this? *(Answer any questions.)* Great, let's review the love languages, and I will give you examples from each one. *(Have students look at the board where you wrote the love languages.)* With each one of these I want you to think to yourself, "Does this make me feel loved, or do I just really like it?"

Okay, the first one is Words of Affirmation. Do you feel loved when people say nice things to you like "Way to Go," "Nice job," "You're the best!" or do you just really like it when people say nice things to you?

The second one is Quality Time. Do you feel loved when people purposefully spend time with you and just you? For example, does it make you feel loved if your mom or dad says, "Let's spend Saturday together, just me and you. We will watch some movies and make lunch together," or do you just really like it when people spend time with you?

The third one is Acts of Service. Do you feel loved when people do things for you? For example, do you feel loved if someone makes your bed, cleans your room, or does your chores for you? Does it make you feel loved when people do things for you, or do you just really like it?

The fourth one is Gifts. Do you feel loved when people give you unexpected gifts? For example, do you feel loved if someone goes out of their way to buy you a gift or makes you something that's really great? Does getting gifts make you feel loved, or do you just really like to get gifts?

Finally, the fifth one is Touch. Do you feel loved through touch? For example, do you feel loved when you sit really close to your mom or dad, get your back rubbed, or get a hug? Does physical contact make you feel loved, or do you just really like it?

These are the five love languages that you have learned about. Now it's time for you to choose the two that make you feel the most loved. First, look at the assessment you completed. If you have two columns that have more x's circled than others, then these are probably your two love languages. Each column from left to right is the same language as I've written on the white board 1–5. If you have ties then look at the ties and try to decide between those and make your best guess. *(Give students enough time to look over their assessment and ask questions.)*

I want you to look at the board and decide on your first choice. Don't say it out loud, just look at the one that is your first choice and memorize the number by it. Has everyone done that? *(Make sure everyone is ready.)* Has everyone memorized the number? Okay, I want everyone to put their head on their desk, and I'm going to have you raise your hand with the number of fingers that represents your first choice. So if words of affirmation is your first choice, I want you to raise your hand with one finger.

TEACHING/PRESENTATION:

1. Write the five love languages on the board in the order that they were taught.

2. Tell class that they will pick their top two love languages.

3. Use ice cream shop illustration.

4. Ask students if they need clarification.

5. When a student picks a love language, that doesn't mean that the teacher will do more for them. For example, students who chose gifts won't get more gifts from teacher.

6. Ask students if they need clarification.

7. Tell students you will be going over the five love languages with examples.

8. Go over the five love languages giving examples in each category. Ask students at the end of each love language, "Does this make you feel loved, or do you just really like it?"

9. It's time for students to pick two.

   • Have them memorize the number next to their first choice.

   • Have them put their head down on desk.

   • Have them hold up number of fingers indicating choice.

   • Record their responses.

   • Repeat the process for secondary choice.

I'm going to write down each person's first choice. Please raise your hands with the number of fingers that represent your first choice now. This is the love language that makes you feel the most loved. *(You may want to do this by rows or however you have them seated so students don't have to keep their hands raised for a long time. Record each student's response. Normally when I'm doing this I say, "Thank you (insert name), you may put your hand down.")* **Thank you, go ahead and raise your heads up.**

Now look at the board again and make your second choice. Memorize the number by your second choice. Does everyone have their second choice memorized? Do you have the number memorized? Okay, go ahead and put your heads on your desk again. Please raise your hand now and show me the number of your second choice. *(Record each student's second choice on the form.)* **Thank you, go ahead and raise your heads up.**

Each of you has chosen your top two love languages. Congratulations! Now let's see what this looks like in our class. I am going to briefly divide you into your groups so you can see who shares your love language as well as who has chosen the other ones. *(Point to various spots in the room where you want each group to stand. For example, say, "If your first choice was words of affirmation, please stand here." Do this for all five love languages.)* **Now that each of you is in your group, take a good look at who else shares your same love language. Isn't it interesting that even though you may have almost nothing else in common with a person in your group, you have the same love language? Now you do have something in common with them.**

Okay, now it's time to divide into our secondary groups. If your second choice is words of affirmation, please go here. *(Point to the words of affirmation group.)* **If your second choice was quality time, please go here.** *(Point to the quality time group.)* **If your second choice was acts of service, please go here.** *(Point to the acts of service group.)* **If your second choice was gifts, please go here.** *(Point to the gifts group.)* **And if your second choice was touch, please go here.** *(Point to the touch group. Nobody should be standing where they were for the first group. Look around and make sure everyone is in a different group.)* **Nobody should be standing where they were for the first group. Has everyone moved to a new group?** *(Make corrections if necessary.)* **Look at the people in your group, who share the same secondary love language with you. Now look around the room and notice who is standing in the group where you just came from. You have something in common with these people. Even though this is the secondary group, you both feel loved in the same way.**

I would like everybody to go back to your seat and sit down. *(After students are seated, hand out the placards. Have students write down their primary and secondary love languages on the placard. Collect the placards and have students sit in a circle, all together on the floor or whatever is customary in your classroom. The idea is to make it more of a personal time for discussion. It's best if each student can see the student who is currently*

10. Students are divided into their love language groups.

11. Teacher points out that even though there may have been previous differences, now they have the love languages in common.

12. Students are divided into their secondary love language groups.

13. Teacher comments on similarities.

14. Students are seated and record their love languages on a placard.

15. Teacher grabs a writing tablet and has class sit in a circle so students can see each other.

16. Tell class this is an opportunity for them to share.

sharing. Also, take a tablet and a pen to record the students' ideas for the final question.) **We are going to have a discussion about your love languages. This is an opportunity for you to share with all of us about your love language adventure. Let me start by asking all of you, "How did you finally figure out what your primary love language is? I mean, did you just instantly know or did something happen that made you realize this was definitely your love language? Briefly tell us about it."** *(Call on a few people, and go to the next question.)* **How do you think knowing your love language will help you at home and at school?** *(Call on as many people as possible.)* **What have you learned about your family and friends after studying the love languages?** *(Call on a few people, and go to the final question.)* **How can we use the love languages in our classroom to make it really great?** *(Try to get everyone to participate. Write the ideas down.)*

CLOSURE:

Thank you for this great discussion. I really like your ideas about how we can use the love languages to make our classroom a better place. I had you write your love languages down so we can attach it to your desk and all of us will remember what makes you feel loved. I think this will make it easier for all of us to practice the ideas suggested today.

As you meet new people, try to figure out what their love language is. Remember you can do this by observing them closely. Being a good listener and asking questions about their life is a great start.

If you don't feel like you are being loved by those who are close to you, talk to them about your love language and try your best to explain what makes you feel loved. Even if they don't choose to love you the way you would like, at least you gave them something to think about. Maybe they have never heard of the love languages.

No matter what, it's really important that you go home and find a time when you can talk to your family about your love languages. I'm sure they will appreciate what you have discovered. You might even have a great conversation about what their love language is, if you haven't already. Knowing the love languages is something you can use for the rest of your life. *(Review the objectives from the white board with class.)*

Thank you for being such a great class. Please go back to your seats.

ASSIGNMENT:

There is no assignment for students. Please read the other chapters for additional information that explains how to use the love language information in your classroom. It has been written for a variety of people. You may find that reading the section for administrators gives you ideas for the classroom. Or if you are an administrator, you may find it useful to read the section written for counselors. What's important is to make the love languages a part of your school's culture on a daily basis.

17. Ask: "How did you finally figure out what your primary love language is? I mean, did you just instantly know or did something happen that made you realize this was definitely your love language? Briefly tell us about it." *(Call on a few people and go to the next question.)*

18. Ask: "How do you think knowing your love language will help you at home and at school?" *(Call on as many people as possible.)*

19. Ask: "What have you learned about your family and friends after studying the love languages?" *(Call on a few people and go to the final question.)*

20. Ask: "How can we use the love languages in our classroom to make it really great?" *(Try to get everyone to participate. Write the ideas down.)*

CLOSURE:

Thank you for this great discussion. I really like your ideas about how we can use the love languages to make our classroom a better place. I had you write your love languages down so we can attach it to your desk and all of us will remember what makes you feel loved. I think this will make it easier for all of us to do some of the ideas suggested today.

As you meet new people try to figure out what their love language is. Remember you can do this by observing them closely. Being a good listener and asking questions about their life is a great start.

If you don't feel like you are being loved by those who are close to you, talk to them about your love language and try your best to explain what makes you feel loved. Even if they don't choose to love you the way you would like, at least you gave them something to think about. Maybe they have never heard of the love languages.

No matter what, it is really important that you go home and find a time when you can talk to your parents about your love languages. I'm sure they will appreciate what you have discovered. You might even have a great conversation about what their love language is, if you haven't already. Knowing the love languages is something you can use for the rest of your life.

Thank you for being such a great class. *(Review objectives written on white board with class.)* Please go back to your seats.

ASSIGNMENT:

None required.

FINAL THOUGHTS

Teaching the final lesson always brings a sense of accomplishment. You have worked hard for weeks, and now the students have a firm foundation and a true definition of love. It may surprise you how much your students like to talk about the love languages. I encourage you to keep this excitement going. The goal is to make it a part of your school culture. Just like their times tables, the love languages are something that students can use for life. Once people have a clear understanding about what the love languages are and how they work, it seems to give them an edge on life. Knowing and using the love languages causes most to see beyond themselves and recognize the needs of others; this is a task that is difficult for adults, let alone children. Amazingly, the love languages enable just that.

Use the love languages every day in practical applications. This is one of the greatest ways to solidify the learning. When you see someone loving someone else with a love language, recognize their effort. Reward students for using the love languages so they become a permanent part of their life. A school culture built around looking out for the needs of others becomes a wonderful place to be. Your school should expect students to use the love languages just as they would expect them to use good manners. Make the love languages a common expression at your school, and all of the other character qualities you desire from students will follow. The love language curriculum has the potential to extend beyond your classroom and affect future classrooms, families, friends, and, someday, spouses. Be the model of love your students deserve.

Thank you for teaching children how to show and receive love. Generations to come will thank you.

FROM THE CLASSROOM

I have taught the love language lessons 360 times. I can honestly say I have never taught a more rewarding curriculum during my entire teaching career. Many of us observed big changes in the attitudes of the students. They hungered for more lessons. The compliments from parents came pouring in weekly. Nothing lifts your spirit more than knowing people not only approve of what you are trying to accomplish, but also see the value in what you are teaching.

The torch has been handed to you. I hope you were able to witness the incredible effect learning the love languages can have on students, family, and staff. I also hope teaching these lessons brightened your day, brought you renewal, and lifted your spirit. May it continue to do so as you make the love languages a part of your everyday life.

It's time to tell others about the great stories from your classroom. I would really like to hear them.

CHAPTER 9

Using the Love Language Information

INTRODUCTION

This chapter is broken down into different categories for various staff members who work in the educational field. As we all know, there are a variety of positions that support any one school. Each staff member who works at a school brings a unique perspective. Let's take a moment and narrowly focus on the different perspectives of educators at any given school or district, keeping in mind the impact they could have by using the love languages.

A counselor or social worker will see a child as someone who needs to be made whole in order to function in the classroom. A teacher will see a child as someone who has great potential for learning and invest terrific amounts of time that will benefit them academically. A principal will see a child as someone who needs to get the best education possible and will surround them with every advantage by providing excellent staff members, structure, and discipline. The school secretary will see a child as someone who needs support by connecting the child with his/her family in areas of daily necessities. The school nurse will see a child as someone who must be physically healthy in order to do well at school. The playground supervisors will see a child as someone who needs safety and an opportunity to play. Educational assistants and specialists will see a child as someone who needs extra help and who has as much potential as anyone else. The school librarian will see a child as an avid reader whose possibilities will be opened wide with books. The custodian will see a child as someone who needs a healthy environment to achieve academic success. The superintendent will see a child as someone who is worthy of investing in and will channel financial resources to make learning possible. The school board will see a child as someone who has the right to learn and to be protected through policies. The parents of a child will see their child as someone they love no matter what happens. A child will see themselves as they perceive others see them.

Reading these next sections should encourage you to network with your colleagues and put into place a system whereby all children are being impacted by the love languages. Even though the three main headings are "Teacher," "Specialists/Support Staff," and "Administrators," you should be able to find information to fit your current job assignment. I encourage everyone to read all three because this will make it easier for different disciplines to work together at making the love languages a part of your school culture.

Making the love languages a part of the school culture will add a lot of depth and meaning to the school itself. Staff and students will enjoy being there more, academic successes will go up because of connections, and inappropriate behaviors will go down. How can I be sure? It's a simple equation: When people feel understood, accepted, and loved, they gain confidence. With confidence comes a willingness to try harder, and this includes overcoming obstacles. These obstacles can be academic, social, or personal. The love languages go beyond simple respect curriculums by building connections between people. Connections create a sense of camaraderie that encourages everyone to work together toward the common goal of success.

TEACHER

The love languages provide the classroom teacher with a base from which she can build connections, expectations, and behaviors. Modeling, supporting, and encouraging their use is essential. Because the classroom teacher has access to the same group of students each day, she/he will get to see dynamics that don't appear anywhere else in the school. Classroom dynamics make for a perfect environment to instruct students on how to behave toward one another. There are opportunities each day for students to hone their skills and think about the needs of others. The classroom teacher can encourage the use of the love languages by rewarding students. Motivation and rewards should be used in such a way that students can make a choice in one of five categories that coincide with the love languages. (See section on Ways to Motivate.)

Academics can be incorporated into the love languages. Some teachers will find that after learning the love languages, students will begin to think on deeper levels. Group discussions can lead to students writing papers that demonstrate their knowledge of the love languages. They can practice in narrative or expository style. Post their work for display.

1. **Encourage Students:** Use positive comments that point out a student who is modeling the love languages.
2. **Reward:** Build a reward system using raffle tickets. When you spot a student using the love languages, place a ticket into a drawing for a weekly prize. Don't remove the tickets for the entire year. The more tickets, the more chances to win. Create rewards that allow students to choose from one of the five love language categories. (See motivating section for ideas.)
3. **Discipline:** Use examples from the love languages when a student isn't acting appropriately. "What do we call it when someone is calling someone else a name?" (Harassment) Focus on bringing the student back to the positive side by discussing behavior and having them tell you what they could do differently.
4. **Group Students:** Throughout the day, break students into groups based on similar or dissimilar love languages. "Find someone to read with whose love language is Touch."
5. **Writing:** Have students do writing assignments that involve the love languages as they learn about new ones each week. Have them make up stories around holidays about people who use the love languages to help others. Post the stories on bulletin boards in the hallways.
6. **Math:** Create charts that show the percentage of students who fall into different categories. Break it down for primary and secondary. If the entire school participates, use this data for an even bigger project.
7. **Special Assignments:** Rotate each week making one of the love languages the focus for the class. Have students pick people in the school they are going to target with the love language of the week. This is done in the same way as the assignments they are familiar with from the love language lessons.
8. **Play Games:** Make up games where students have to group students in their class according to love languages.

SPECIALISTS/SUPPORT STAFF

The love languages are the perfect starting point for anyone who deals with the psychological side of students. Knowing students' love languages can give insight into what is causing their behaviors. Students who aren't having their love language needs met often gravitate toward support staff. When students frequently need to be near support staff, they may be living in fear that they will no longer be loved in the way that makes them feel loved. Divorce, moving, and fighting are typical causes for these fears.

If students in your school have gone through the love language lessons and are frequently accessing the counselor, social worker, or nurse, ask them to tell you what their love languages are. Use this as a starting point to discover if there are any deficits or perceived deficits. Offer students guidance for overcoming their feelings of not being loved.

Be ready for students to disclose information after the lesson on Touch. As they become aware that certain actions are inappropriate, they may seek out support staff after the lessons. If a counselor or nurse suspects a child wants to talk about abuse, use the love languages as a safe starting point. Questions may sound like, "Do you remember the lesson on Touch? What did you think about that?" This approach can be used for anyone you suspect may have been abused. The love languages open a lot of doors for specialists who need to have full and honest discussions with students regarding their behaviors.

1. **Identify:** At the beginning of a counseling session, identify a student's specific love language.
2. **Issues:** For students dealing with a variety of issues including depression, friendship, family, and self-esteem, investigate love language deficits and discuss options for relief.
3. **Parents:** Help parents to understand their child's unique love language and how to love him/her in a more meaningful way. Encourage them to read the The 5 Love Languages of Children, and other books by Gary Chapman to improve their marriage and family life.
4. **Educational Staff:** Help staff members understand what motivates students with whom they are working. Use the love languages as a primary foundation.
5. **Data Base:** Keep a computer database of all the students who go through the love language lessons. Record their love languages for future reference.
6. **Continuing Education:** Keep the love languages fresh by going back to the classrooms and doing "mini" lessons. Encourage the students to use the love language terminology.

ADMINISTRATORS

Administrators will find that many of the students they work with will have love language deficits. Using the love languages to determine if a student is acting out because they don't feel loved is very beneficial. Oftentimes, students won't perform in a classroom because they don't feel a connection with the teacher. An administrator can sit with a staff member, student, or both and discuss what it would take to make connections using the love languages.

Behavior contracts work best when the student is motivated. Build contracts with a reward for good behavior that coincides with the student's love language. Have discussions with students that lead them to the behaviors and expectations you are looking for. Use negative behavior terminology to explain the inappropriate behaviors you are seeing.

Modeling the love languages to staff and students means a lot to those who work for you. Use the love language terminology on a regular basis in your school and create an expected school climate. The message it will send to students, staff, and parents is, "We are a school that cares about the whole person, and our desire is to make positive connections with those around us as we work together toward success." Incorporating the love languages into your school and putting them into practice makes this message real. The love language curriculum documents that a school cares about the whole student and gives students the tools they need to access support if they are being mistreated.

1. **Curriculum:** Make the love language curriculum available to all staff.
2. **Staff Development:** In-service your staff on how to use the love languages at school. Encourage them to use it as a motivator for students. Have other love language books available for them to check out for personal use.
3. **Teach:** Be one of the love language lesson presenters.
4. **Discipline:** Use illustrations from the love languages when working with inappropriate behavior. Harassment, isolation, bullying, bribery, and inappropriate touch are all familiar topics to the students after the lessons have been taught. Discuss with students how they have crossed the personal safety line and offer suggestions for appropriate behavior using the love languages.
5. **Set the Tone:** Have a love language day/week where all students wear badges that say what their love languages are. Have the older students teach the younger students.
6. **Intercom:** Make announcements for the day with a saying that connects to a love language. Offer suggestions for students to practice a love language for the day.
7. **Database:** Have a database of the students' love languages. Use the information to guide parents and staff when dealing with students. Use a school-wide database to see how the school breaks down by percentages. Look for trends. Do the same for classrooms. (See Data section.)

DATA

Having student data can be useful for looking at trends and drawing conclusions. For example, classroom data can be used as one more source of information when placing students in a teacher's classroom for the following year. If a class has too many Quality Time and/or Words of Affirmation students, then the teacher will feel exhausted on a daily basis. Both of these groups tend to delight in having the teacher's regular attention. Keeping the love languages divided equally when placing students creates a nice balance.

In my school, I recorded every student's love language on an Excel spreadsheet and created graphs and charts. It was relatively easy to do and didn't take much time to enter the information. I passed on the information I thought would be interesting and useful to the teachers and principal. Teachers received information from me that included pie charts for a specific class, for the grade level, and for the entire school. I also provided a class roster with the students' primary and secondary love languages. Administrators received three pie charts as well, for the entire school, the entire school with boys vs. girls, and grade levels.

If a class or school is evenly dispersed then there aren't a lot of conclusions to draw. However, if the data is skewed, showing, for example, that the majority of the school leans more heavily toward one specific love language, then strategic programs can be put into place. When I use the term "programs," I am referring to something as simple as increasing parent volunteers so students get more individual attention. Here are some ideas for administrators and support staff to consider if the overall school leans heavily toward one particular love language.

SCHOOL-WIDE IMPLEMENTATIONS

If a school leans heavily toward . . .

Words of Affirmation:
1. School hallways need lots of positive environmental print.
2. All staff members need to verbally acknowledge students more, even if they aren't from their class.
3. Letters and phone calls to home should be made recognizing good behaviors.
4. Public recognition can occur at assemblies for individuals, classes, or grade levels.
5. Activities for students that will afford them the opportunity to be praised regardless of skill level might be implemented.

Quality Time:
1. Increase volunteers to provide more individual attention.
2. Sit with students during lunchtime.
3. Go out to recess and participate during activities.
4. Memorize student names and use them when possible.

5. Take a moment to ask students about themselves or other interests besides school-related ones.

6. Increase programs and activities where students can work alongside adults.

7. Offer principal luncheons as a reward.

Acts of Service:

1. Increase volunteers to provide more academic services such as tutoring.

2. Offer incentives for students to serve other students during lunch, such as wiping tables, throwing away trash, or even bringing lunches to students at their table. A Waiter-for-the-Week type of program might be used, for example.

3. Have all staff look for more opportunities to help students with little things (having an assistance attitude).

4. Playground supervisors can help students resolve conflicts, set up games, and make sure equipment is tops. "Let me put more air in that ball for you."

Gifts:

1. Recognize birthdays in the office by announcing them over the PA and having students come to the office to receive a little gift, e.g., coupons, pencils, or little plastic toys.

2. Have programs that offer tangible rewards for good behavior.

3. Offer principal luncheons as a reward, asking students specifically what they would like to order.

Touch:

1. Greet students with handshakes and high fives.

2. Pat students on the back between shoulder blades when opportunity arises.

3. Encourage PE teachers to increase activities where there is more physical contact, e.g., games where tagging is required, or dance.

4. Increase adult supervision for safety during free times. Note: There's a high probability that students will engage in above-average physical contact during free times, e.g., wrestling, pushing, and general horseplay, which may lead to disciplinary action.

WAYS TO MOTIVATE IN THE CLASSROOM

Let the reader understand, these suggestions are not to be done all the time or simply with one student. Hopefully it is obvious that if the room was conducted like that, the attempts would be thought of as trite, and jealousy would ensue. Motivating with the love languages needs to be sincere, direct, and intentional. Everyone should feel loved equally in their own language. Use some type of easy record-keeping system to make sure you are attempting to love all students equally. A good rule of thumb is: Not so much that they take you for granted, not so little that they can't remember the last time you tried.

Words of Affirmation:

1. Verbal praise (general): "Nice Job!"
2. Verbal compliment (specific): "I really like how you took the time to write a story that keeps the reader interested. I learned a lot about whales."
3. Notes to students expressing praise.
4. Letters home recognizing specific accomplishments.
5. Using students' names when calling on them.
6. Recognizing accomplishments publicly during class meetings, assemblies, etc.
7. Greeting students by name outside of the classroom.
8. Posting work on bulletin boards with teacher's positive comments.

Quality Time:

1. Ask individual students if they would be willing to share a story with you about a life experience.
2. Spend time interviewing students about academic goals and objectives.
3. Be a good listener.
4. Offer to allow students a chance to work occasionally on projects/tasks with you.
5. Sit with students at lunch.
6. Go out to recess with students once in a while.
7. Increase parent volunteers to provide more individual attention.
8. If students are younger, have older students be their buddies and listen to them read.

Acts of Service:

1. Help a student find a lost item.
2. Help them understand a complicated problem by sitting down with them (inconspicuously) and explaining the procedure.
3. In general look for opportunities to assist the student when it's obvious to you and to him that you are going out of your way to help. Never begrudgingly!

Gifts:

1. Have prizes available for successful students.
2. Know a gift person's secondary language and use that as well, since gifts can be hard to give throughout a typical day.
3. Create a reward system with tangible items available.
4. Ask them what they received from their family after a special occasion, e.g., birthday, Christmas, etc.
5. Celebrate all students' birthdays with a little trinket.

Touch:

1. Stand at the door and greet students with a handshake each morning as they enter the room. Use this opportunity to teach them firm grips and eye contact.
2. High-five or fist-bump.
3. Pat on the back between the shoulder blades.

Dear Parent(s):

I am excited to inform you about a fantastic curriculum your student will be learning. It's called *Discovering the 5 Love Languages*. It teaches students how to identify what makes them feel loved, as well as how to identify what makes others feel loved. These concepts are based on Dr. Gary Chapman's #1 *New York Times* bestseller *The 5 Love Languages*.

The five love languages will be taught over several weeks with one new language being revealed each week. Each lesson will explore one of the love languages listed below and will also discuss its opposite. Here is a summary of the lessons:

1. Words of Affirmation vs. Harassment
2. Quality Time vs. Leaving People Out
3. Acts of Service vs. Bullying
4. Gifts vs. Bribery
5. Safe Touch vs. Unsafe Touch (Personal Safety)

Many students who go through these lessons say they feel closer to their family, friends, and teacher. It is our desire to have a school where students are making connections and are actively engaged in good citizenship. We want to educate the whole child! Studies have shown that students who make connections with others tend to perform much better academically.

We would like to encourage you to discuss with your child each week what they have learned to reinforce the concepts. The Academic Focus Pages (AFP) your child will be filling out, which coincide with the lessons, have special areas on them titled "Home Connection Section." These sections of the pages have been highlighted for easy reference, and they represent an area of significant importance to review with your child.

You may find yourself intrigued by what your child is learning and want more information. I would be more than happy to share with you the titles of other books that have been written on an adult level.

Thank you for embarking on this adventure with us. If I can answer any questions please feel free to contact me.

Sincerely,

Common Core State Standards and CCR Alignment

(Standards for English Language Arts (ELA): Speaking and Listening—Grades 1–6)

Discovering the 5 Love Languages: Lessons align with 29/36 Common Core State Standards (CCSS) in the area of Speaking and Listening and College Career Readiness (CCR) for grades 1–6. Alignment could extend further if the instructor chooses to use additional lesson supports such as writing stories. For the purpose of this documentation, the focus is simply based on what is directly taught in the lessons themselves, "as is."

Common Core State Standards describes Speaking and Listening as:

Including but not limited to skills necessary for formal presentations, the Speaking and Listening standards require students to develop a range of broadly useful oral communication and interpersonal skills. Students must learn to work together, express and listen carefully to ideas, integrate information from oral, visual, quantitative, and media sources, evaluate what they hear, use media and visual displays strategically to help achieve communicative purposes, and adapt speech to context and task.[1]

The lessons are highly interactive and meet most of the common core requirements for Speaking and Listening throughout with a strong emphasis on collaboration. Some of the thirty-six standards weren't listed when they

---

[1] National Governors Association Center for Best Practices, Council of Chief State School Officers, Common Core State Standards (Speaking and Listening), Publisher: National Governors Association Center for Best Practices, Council of Chief State School Officers, Washington D.C., 2010, 8.

potentially could have been in an attempt to be conservative. For example, *Discovering the 5 Love Languages* lessons don't require any media sources or visual displays for students (at certain grade levels) to present their ideas. A case could be made that when students draw symbols/pictures on their Academic Focus Pages and share them with the classroom, this could be considered a form of visual presentation. Rather than having to justify those types of situations, every effort has been made to identify the standards in which no case need be made for alignment. Ultimately it is up to the educator to decide what aligns based on how they teach but the alignments listed below should be easy to identify within the lessons. They have been listed by grade level and individual lesson for quick reference.

ENGLISH LANGUAGE ARTS (ELA) COMMON CORE STANDARDS— GRADE LEVEL ALIGNMENT
[SPEAKING AND LISTENING]

First Grade:
SL. 1.1 a-c, 1.2, 1.3, 1.4, 1.5, 1.6 and corresponding (CCR's)

Second Grade:
SL. 2.1 a-c, 2.2, 2.3, 2.4, 2.5, 2.6 and corresponding (CCR's)

Third Grade:
SL. 3.1 a-d, 3.2, 3.3, 3.4, 3.6 and corresponding (CCR's)

Fourth Grade:
SL. 4.1 a-d, 4.2, 4.3, 4.4 and corresponding (CCR's)

Fifth Grade:
SL. 5.1 a-d, 5.2, 5.3, 5.4 and corresponding (CCR's)

Sixth Grade:
SL. 6.1 a-d, 6.2, 6.3, 6.4 and corresponding (CCR's)

ENGLISH LANGUAGE ARTS (ELA) COMMON CORE STATE STANDARDS— LESSON ALIGNMENT
[SPEAKING AND LISTENING]

Lesson 1: The True Meaning of Love

SL. 1.1 a-c, 1.2, 1.3, 1.4, 1.5, 1.6

SL. 2.1 a-c, 2.2, 2.3, 2.4, 2.6

SL. 3.1 b-d, 3.2, 3.3, 3.4, 3.6

SL. 4.1 b-d, 4.2, 4.3

SL. 5.1 b-d, 5.2, 5.4

SL. 6.1 c-d, 6.2, 6.3, 6.4

Lesson 2: Words of Affirmation

SL. 1.1 a-c, 1.2, 1.3, 1.4, 1.5, 1.6

SL. 2.1 a-c, 2.2, 2.3, 2.4, 2.6

SL. 3.1 b-d, 3.2, 3.3, 3.4, 3.6

SL. 4.1 b-d, 4.2, 4.3

SL. 5.1 b-d, 5.2, 5.4

SL. 6.1 c-d, 6.2, 6.3, 6.4

Lesson 3: Quality Time

SL. 1.1 a-c, 1.2, 1.3, 1.4, 1.5, 1.6

SL. 2.1 a-c, 2.2, 2.3, 2.4, 2.6

SL. 3.1 b-d, 3.2, 3.3, 3.4, 3.6

SL. 4.1 b-d, 4.2, 4.3, 4.4

SL. 5.1 b-d, 5.2, 5.4

SL. 6.1 c-d, 6.2, 6.3, 6.4

Lesson 4: Acts of Service

SL. 1.1 a-c, 1.2, 1.3, 1.4, 1.6

SL. 2.1 a-c, 2.2, 2.3, 2.4, 2.6

SL. 3.1 b-d, 3.2, 3.3, 3.6

SL. 4.1 b-d, 4.2, 4.3

SL. 5.1 b-d, 5.2

SL. 6.1 c-d, 6.2, 6.3, 6.4

Lesson 5: Gifts

SL. 1.1 a-c, 1.2, 1.3, 1.4, 1.6

SL. 2.1 a-c, 2.2, 2.3, 2.4, 2.6

SL. 3.1 b-d, 3.2, 3.3, 3.4, 3.6

SL. 4.1 b-d, 4.2, 4.3, 4.4

SL. 5.1 b-d, 5.2, 5.3

SL. 6.1 b-d, 6.2, 6.3

Lesson 6: Touch

SL. 1.1 a-c, 1.2, 1.3, 1.4

SL. 2.1 a-c, 2.2, 2.3

SL. 3.1 b-d, 3.2, 3.3, 3.6

SL. 4.1 b-d, 4.2, 4.3

SL. 5.1 b-d, 5.2

SL. 6.1 b-d, 6.2, 6.3, 6.4

Lesson 7: Choosing Your Love Languages

SL. 1.1 a-c, 1.2, 1.3, 1.4

SL. 2.1 a-c, 2.2, 2.3, 2.4,

SL. 3.1 a-d, 3.2, 3.3, 3.4, 3.6

SL. 4.1 a-d, 4.2, 4.3, 4.4

SL. 5.1 a-d, 5.2, 5.3

SL. 6.1 a-d, 6.2, 6.4

How to Use the Academic Focus Pages

These pages have been designed to help students reach deeper levels of thinking. The lesson objectives will be enhanced through the strategies provided. The majority of the strategies are research-based to help you (the instructor) and your classroom think deeper and reach higher levels of academic excellence and achievement. It will also create strong academic connections between you and your students. Each lesson from the book has two pages (typically), which coincide with and support the lessons being taught. Students will have opportunities to work with cues, questions, advance organizers, compare/contrast, nonlinguistic representations, set objectives, summarizing/note-taking, and reflection.

Ideally, it is best practice for students to have the "Notes and Reflection Journal" page available to them from the beginning of each lesson. Summarizing/note-taking requires students to sift through, analyze, and decide which information is important enough for later use. Summarizing/note-taking is an invaluable strategy that spans across all content areas and advances academic achievement. Be aware, however, that students do not come by note-taking naturally and will require your specific instruction to develop a strategy. The space for note-taking has been purposely limited to encourage students to write only that which is truly essential.

The second half of the Notes and Reflections Journal is concerned with reflecting. This half of the page helps students apply the lesson objectives that you wrote on the white board. By having them set personal goals/skills for using the information, they will be able to make the lessons meaningful. You will find that this fits in nicely with the homework assignments at the end of each lesson where students are asked to extend what they know into "real-life" settings such as school and home. Students should be encouraged to refer back to the reflections section and use that to help them carry out their homework assignments.

The Notes and Reflections Journal is written generically, giving you the opportunity to have students fill in the lesson title and lesson number each time you teach. Whether you have the students alternate the Notes and Reflections Journal page with each Academic Focus Page (AFP) or just create a separate journal with Notes and Reflections Journal pages is up to you. Depending on how your school plans on using the AFPs overall for building school climate, you could:

1. Let students keep the Notes and Reflections Journal at their desk for reference to homework assignments and collect only the AFPs.
2. Collect all pages each time and make a collection of work to present to parents at conference time. Send the collection home with parents.
3. Send all work home each time a lesson is taught (not advised).
4. Make copies of AFPs or send originals to the next year's teacher for students to compare their growth at the end of the two-year cycle (advised). Have students take both collections of work home at the end of the school year.
5. Any other options that you can think of that would work well for you, your students, and their families.

The goal of these lessons is to discover the five love languages. I find it more interesting and intriguing for students when they "discover" a new love language during each lesson. This also serves to keep them focused on the set objectives for that day. I suggest handing out the new AFP each time you teach the lesson rather than making a giant collection of pages for them to work from. I'm also a big fan of making copies of the AFPs and journal pages so that you are able to send the original work home for parents to review with their child. I like copies so that I can send them on to the specialists who also work closely with the students. There are always students who need extra intervention strategies and support. Counselors, school nurses, and principals will appreciate knowing how to encourage and motivate a student. It's great insight for offering suggestions to the student or parent(s).

Finally, let's not forget assessment. Good instruction and materials allow the teacher to determine a student's achievement level and make adjustments when needed. Using these pages, an instructor can check for understanding, look for areas of concern, and guide students to make better connections with other students, their family members, and, of course, you. Each AFP or journal page should be carefully reviewed after completion, especially in regard to the personal safety lessons. Students may disclose information that reveals a crisis in their lives, and your assistance may be required.

If you are able to print all of the pages for your students, I think you will be pleased with the outcome. Each student will have completed pages that are meaningful and great for reflecting. The same lesson pages are purposefully taught for two years, back to back. This solidifies understanding and gives students the opportunity to compare and contrast the differences from one year to the next.

Further, as I mentioned earlier, the completed work can be used when visiting with parents during student conferences. Teaching the love language lessons provides valuable information and insight that can be shared with parents and may help them better understand how to connect with their child at home. The topic itself is a positive one and could be a great way to break the ice with your parents as you start any conference session, let alone a difficult one.

In the end, the important thing is that students learn how to show and receive love. That they are enabled to make significant connections with those closest in their lives. As we know from the research presented in this book, there's plenty to suggest that students who feel connected with people in their lives have a leg up toward academic achievement, friendship, resiliency, and life.

Good luck to you and your students as you discover the five love languages together!

Discovering the 5 Love Languages

"A life changing experience!"

 Words of Affirmation

 Quality Time

 Acts of Service

 Gifts

 Safe Touch

THE TRUE MEANING OF "LOVE"

Let's get started!

1. Draw a picture of you and your family doing something that makes you feel truly loved.

Use words or sentences to explain WHY this makes you feel loved:

_____

_____

_____

_____

_____

Name _____ Date _____

 WORDS OF AFFIRMATION

○ *Makes me feel loved.*
○ *I like it.*

1. **Words of Affirmation** are truthful words that are spoken or written from one person to another that will uplift them and can make them feel good, encouraged, or loved. Think of five words that you could use in a sentence that would make people feel good, encouraged, or loved and write them in the bubbles. An example has been done for you!

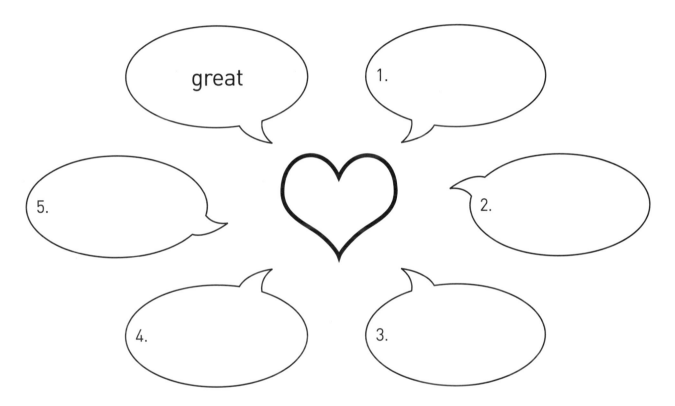

great

1.

5.

2.

4.

3.

Use each word that you wrote above in a sentence to make someone feel good.
*Example: You are a **great** friend!*

1. _____

2. _____

3. _____

4. _____

5. _____

WORDS OF AFFIRMATION

∽ *Opposite* ∽

1.

"Harassment"

Do you know what this word means?

Yes   or   No

DEFINITION OVER HERE!

Hurtful words said to a person over and over again that make them feel bad or hurt their feelings.

2. Write a sentence using the word "harassment."

_____

_____

_____

3. Draw a face of what you think a person looks like when they hear nice words:

4. Draw a face of what you think a person looks like when they get harassed:

5. How well do you know what "harassment" means now that you've done this lesson?

A. _____ I really understand what harassment means!

B. _____ I kind of understand what harassment means.

C. _____ I still don't understand what harassment is.

Name _____   Date _____

 QUALITY TIME

○ *Makes me feel loved.*
○ *I like it.*

1. Draw a picture of you spending quality time with your friend.

[ ]

2. Write a sentence describing what you are doing in the picture above.

_____

_____

_____

3. Draw a picture of someone not being included with another person during an activity.

[ ]

4. How do they feel being left out? _____

Name _____ Date _____

ACTS OF SERVICE

○ *Makes me feel loved.*
○ *I like it.*

An **Act of Service** is doing something nice for someone that they don't expect you to do.

WHAT ARE SOME ACTS OF SERVICE YOU CAN DO FOR YOUR:

PARENTS

FRIENDS

BROTHER

SISTER

TEACHER

OTHERS

ACTS OF SERVICE

1. The definition of **Acts of Service** is to do something kind for others by helping them out. The opposite would be doing something cruel to others or hurting them in some way. This could be verbally, emotionally, or physically. We call this negative behavior "bullying."

WHAT WOULD YOU DO TO STOP A BULLY?

A. I would tell them to _____ in a serious voice.

B. I would _____ or _____ away from the person.

C. If the person still follows me I would tell them to _____ in a serious voice.

D. If they continue to follow or bother me I would tell _____.

OUR SCHOOL TAKES SAFETY SERIOUSLY!
HERE IS A TEST TO SEE IF YOU KNOW SOME UNUSUAL FACTS ABOUT BULLYING.

TRUE or FALSE   If I see a bully hurting someone else, I should ignore it because it isn't really hurting me.

TRUE or FALSE   Sending a cruel text message could be a form of bullying.

TRUE or FALSE   If someone bullies a person in the neighborhood, it's not really the school's concern.

TRUE or FALSE   Bullies are always physically bigger than the person they are bullying.

ALWAYS REPORT BULLYING OR ANY DANGEROUS ACTIVITY to an adult. At school, this can be your teacher or anyone else who works at the school. At home, this can be any adult who is a family member, relative, or guardian.

STOP BULLIES! ALWAYS TELL SOMEONE!

GRADES 1 & 2

GIFTS

○ *Makes me feel loved.*
○ *I like it.*

1.

GIFTS I
REALLY WANT!

2. Why did you pick these gifts? Pick one gift and tell us why you picked it.

_____

_____

_____

/ /

BRIBERY
HOME CONNECTION SECTION

Bribery is a negative behavior. It means that someone is trying to give a gift to get you to do something or get something from you. You should always ask your parents' permission before receiving a gift. If someone wants to give you a gift and you don't have permission then follow these three simple steps:

A. Politely refuse the gift by saying, "No, thank you." Tell them that your parents don't allow you to take gifts or money without their permission.

B. Tell your parents that someone offered you a gift.

C. If someone in a car tries to offer you a gift to go with them, scream and run away. Try to find help. Do not spend any time talking to them and don't get close to their car.

GRADES 1 & 2

Name _____ Date _____

 SAFE TOUCH

○ *Makes me feel loved.*
○ *I like it.*

1. In each of the bubbles there is a type of touch. You can write one name or several names inside a bubble of people who make you feel good or loved with that type of touch. For example, you could write dad, mom, brother, sister, friend, or anyone else you can think of.

Hug	Wrestling	Handshake
Kiss	Back Scratch	Tickle
Back Rub	High Five	Pat on the Back
Snuggling	Foot Rub	Fist Bump

2. Can you think of three other touches we didn't name?

/ /

HOME CONNECTION SECTION

Everybody has a different comfort level when it comes to touch. Some people like to be touched and some people don't. Some people only like certain people to touch them. All people have a right to choose who is allowed to enter their personal space. We need to be respectful of a person's personal space even if their love language is Touch.

GRADES 1 & 2

TOUCH (PERSONAL SAFETY)

1. What are the three types of touch? (Hint: one of them is a "not safe" behavior)

   A. _____

   B. _____

   C. _____

2. If **unsafe** touch is going to happen to a child, it's usually done by someone they:

   A. _____

   B. _____

   C. _____

3. What are some reasons a child may not tell someone if a person they know, trust, or love touches them in an **unsafe** way?

   A. _____   B. _____

   C. _____   D. _____

   E. _____   F. _____

4. Who is the first person most kids tell when something bad happens to them?

   _____ but they should tell _____

5. If someone touches you or a friend in an **unsafe way**, you always need to tell at least two adults:

   A. An adult who lives in your _____.

   B. And an adult who works at _____.

Here are some good tips to be safe:
- Avoid situations where you might have to be alone with someone that you feel uneasy about. Tell your parents privately that you don't want to be with them.
- Follow your instincts. If it doesn't seem right then don't do it.
- If someone is bothering you, tell them to "Stop!" and draw your personal safety line.
- If you aren't sure about someone's behavior, ask your parents or an adult at school.

And remember, it's not likely to happen to you, so don't be afraid of everybody and everything. These lessons are to teach you how to be wise and safe!

GRADES 1 & 2

Name _____ Date _____

CHOOSING YOUR LOVE LANGUAGE
(ASSESSMENT)

For the following questions, statements, and actions circle the (x) if it makes you feel loved:

	WORDS OF AFFIRMATION	QUALITY TIME	ACTS OF SERVICE	GIFTS	SAFE TOUCH
HUGS					X
YOU ARE AMAZING	X				
I BOUGHT THIS FOR YOU				X	
I DID YOUR CHORES			X		
WANT TO HANG OUT AFTER SCHOOL?		X			
I MADE THIS FOR YOU				X	
YOU LOOK GREAT TODAY	X				
HIGH FIVE					X
I WILL CLEAN YOUR BEDROOM			X		
LET'S GO TO THE MOVIES		X			
GETTING YOUR BACK RUBBED					X
LET ME HELP YOU			X		
HAPPY BIRTHDAY				X	
THAT'S REALLY COOL	X				
WANT TO COME OVER TO MY HOUSE?		X			
GREAT JOB	X				
I KNEW YOU COLLECTED THESE, SO I BOUGHT ONE FOR YOU				X	
LET'S PLAY TOGETHER AT RECESS		X			
I LOADED THE DISHWASHER FOR YOU			X		
FIST BUMP					X
TOTAL OF X'S CIRCLED					

GRADES 1 & 2

Discovering the 5 Love Languages

"A life changing experience!"

 Words of Affirmation

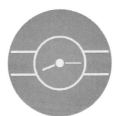 Quality Time

 Acts of Service

 Gifts

 Safe Touch

Name _____ Date _____

THE TRUE MEANING OF "LOVE"

Let's get started!

1. **Do you think all people feel loved in the same way?** (Write a sentence or two explaining why or why not.)

_____

_____

_____

_____

_____

2. **Who makes you feel truly loved?** (In the five circles below put the names of five people who truly make you feel loved. If you can't think of five, then write as many as you can.)

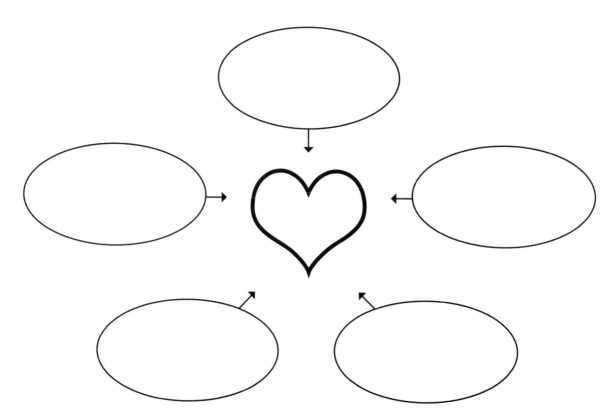

WORDS OF AFFIRMATION

○ *Makes me feel loved.*
○ *I like it.*

∽ *Love Language* ∽

1. **Words of Affirmation** are truthful words that are spoken or written from one person to another that will uplift them and can make them feel good, encouraged, or loved. Think of words, phrases, or a sentence you could say or write to the people listed below that would make them feel good, encouraged, or loved:

A **friend** you are watching play a sport:_____

A **family member** after he/she made your favorite dessert:_____

_____

A **family member** after a bad day at work:_____

_____

Your **teacher**: _____

_____

∽ *Opposite* ∽

2. **Harassment** hurts people's feelings and makes them feel bad. What would school be like if harassment *were* allowed? Fill the boxes with words, symbols, or pictures to describe how students and teachers would feel.

WORDS

sad

SYMBOLS OR PICTURE

☹

 **QUALITY TIME**

○ *Makes me feel loved.*
○ *I like it.*

1. When you are trying to love someone with **Quality Time**, you are intentionally and deliberately being around them to make them feel loved by giving them your time. Pretend that you want to make someone feel loved by spending time with them. What types of quality time activities would you do with them to make them feel loved?

_____

_____

_____

_____

_____

HOW TO HELP SOMEBODY WHO FEELS LEFT OUT
(A "HOW-TO" COMIC STRIP)

2. Nobody wants to feel left out. Imagine that you are on the playground, at the park, or in your neighborhood and you notice that there is a kid who is being left out. Create a mini-comic strip using the information that you just learned. Help other kids understand what they can do to make him/her feel included. (You can use more paper if your teacher allows it.)

Name _____ Date _____

ACTS OF SERVICE

○ *Makes me feel loved.*
○ *I like it.*

1. An **Act of Service** is doing something nice for someone that is intentional, is unexpected, and helps them out. Read the items below and circle the ones that you think are an Act of Service:

> doing your chores;   taking a meal to a friend's house;   doing your brother's or sister's chores;
>
> raking leaves at your neighbor's house without getting paid;   cleaning your bedroom;
>
> doing the dishes at a friend's house;   watering the plants for a neighbor to earn money;
>
> passing out papers for your teacher;   brushing your teeth;   brushing your dog's teeth;
>
> taking care of the neighbor's pets for free;   making breakfast for your parents.

THINKING ABOUT WHAT OTHERS DO FOR US!

2. Take a moment to think about what others do for you. Hopefully this will help you to be thankful! You may be surprised at all of the Acts of Service people do for you that you weren't even aware of. Use the boxes below to write Acts of Service people do for you.

PARENTS

FRIENDS

SCHOOL STAFF

ALL OTHERS

Name _____ Date _____

ACTS OF SERVICE

1. The definition of **Acts of Service** is to do something kind for others by helping them out. The opposite would be doing something cruel to others or hurting them in some way. This could be verbally, emotionally, or physically. We call this negative behavior "bullying."

WHAT WOULD YOU DO TO STOP A BULLY?

A. I would tell them to _____ in a serious voice.

B. I would _____ or _____ away from the person.

C. If the person still follows me I would tell them to _____ in a serious voice.

D. If they continue to follow or bother me I would tell _____.

OUR SCHOOL TAKES SAFETY SERIOUSLY!
HERE IS A TEST TO SEE IF YOU KNOW SOME UNUSUAL FACTS ABOUT BULLYING.

TRUE or FALSE   If I see a bully hurting someone else, I should ignore it because it isn't really hurting me.

TRUE or FALSE   Sending a cruel text message could be a form of bullying.

TRUE or FALSE   If someone bullies a person in the neighborhood, it's not really the school's concern.

TRUE or FALSE   Bullies are always physically bigger than the person they are bullying.

ALWAYS REPORT BULLYING OR ANY DANGEROUS ACTIVITY to an adult. At school, this can be your teacher or anyone else who works at the school. At home, this can be any adult who is a family member, relative, or guardian.

STOP BULLIES! ALWAYS TELL SOMEONE!

GRADES 3 & 4

 **GIFTS**

○ *Makes me feel loved.*
○ *I like it.*

1. If you could have ANY gift in the world, what would it be and why?

_____

_____

_____

DRAW A PICTURE OF YOUR GIFT AND LABEL IT

/ /

BRIBERY
HOME CONNECTION SECTION

Bribery is a negative behavior. It means that someone is trying to give a gift to get you to do something or get something from you. You should always ask your parents' permission before receiving a gift. If someone wants to give you a gift and you don't have permission then follow these three simple steps:

A. Politely refuse the gift by saying, "No, thank you." Tell them that your parents don't allow you to take gifts or money without their permission.

B. Tell your parents that someone offered you a gift.

C. If someone in a car tries to offer you a gift to go with them, scream and run away. Try to find help. Do not spend any time talking to them and don't get close to their car.

GRADES 3 & 4

Name _____ Date _____

 **SAFE TOUCH**

○ *Makes me feel loved.*
○ *I like it.*

WHO CONNECTS WITH YOU?

1. Draw a line from a type of touch on the left to the people who connect with you using that touch on the right. You may be surprised that some of these are considered touch. It's okay if you don't have a lot of lines; everyone is different.

HINT:
Use a different colored pencil for each box of people.

| Hug |
| Kiss on the cheek |
| Back rub |
| Foot rub |
| Pat on the back |
| Snuggling |
| Wrestling |
| High five |
| Head rub |
| Sitting close |
| Holding hands |

GRANDFATHER GRANDMOTHER

BROTHER SISTER

DAD MOM

AUNT UNCLE

OTHER RELATIVE OR FRIEND

WHAT IS APPROPRIATE?

2. From the list of touches above, write the ones you think would be appropriate at school. If the teacher were to ask you, "Why do you think the touches you chose are appropriate at school?" could you support your answers with evidence that makes sense?

_____

_____

/ /

HOME CONNECTION SECTION

Everybody has a different comfort level when it comes to touch. Some people like to be touched and some people don't. Some people only like certain people to touch them. All people have a right to choose what their comfort level is. We need to be respectful of a person's personal space, even if their love language is Touch.

GRADES 3 & 4

TOUCH (PERSONAL SAFETY)

1. What are the three types of touch? (Hint: one of them is a "not safe" behavior)

    A. _____

    B. _____

    C. _____

2. If **unsafe** touch is going to happen to a child, it's usually done by someone they:

    A. _____

    B. _____

    C. _____

3. What are some reasons a child may not tell someone if a person they know, trust, or love touches them in an **unsafe** way?

    A. _____   B. _____

    C. _____   D. _____

    E. _____   F. _____

4. Who is the first person most kids tell when something bad happens to them?

    _____ but they should tell _____

5. If someone touches you or a friend in an **unsafe way**, you always need to tell at least two adults:

    A. An adult who lives in your _____.

    B. And an adult who works at _____.

Here are some good tips to be safe:
- Avoid situations where you might have to be alone with someone that you feel uneasy about. Tell your parents privately that you don't want to be with them.
- Follow your instincts. If it doesn't seem right then don't do it.
- If someone is bothering you, tell them to "Stop!" and draw your personal safety line.
- If you aren't sure about someone's behavior, ask your parents or an adult at school.

And remember, it's not likely to happen to you, so don't be afraid of everybody and everything. These lessons are to teach you how to be wise and safe!

GRADES 3 & 4

CHOOSING YOUR LOVE LANGUAGE
(ASSESSMENT)

For the following questions, statements, and actions circle the (x) if it makes you feel loved:

	WORDS OF AFFIRMATION	QUALITY TIME	ACTS OF SERVICE	GIFTS	SAFE TOUCH
HUGS					X
YOU ARE AMAZING	X				
I BOUGHT THIS FOR YOU				X	
I DID YOUR CHORES			X		
WANT TO HANG OUT AFTER SCHOOL?		X			
I MADE THIS FOR YOU				X	
YOU LOOK GREAT TODAY	X				
HIGH FIVE					X
I WILL CLEAN YOUR BEDROOM			X		
LET'S GO TO THE MOVIES		X			
GETTING YOUR BACK RUBBED					X
LET ME HELP YOU			X		
HAPPY BIRTHDAY				X	
THAT'S REALLY COOL	X				
WANT TO COME OVER TO MY HOUSE?		X			
GREAT JOB	X				
I KNEW YOU COLLECTED THESE, SO I BOUGHT ONE FOR YOU				X	
LET'S PLAY TOGETHER AT RECESS		X			
I LOADED THE DISHWASHER FOR YOU			X		
FIST BUMP					X
TOTAL OF X'S CIRCLED					

Discovering the 5 Love Languages

"A life changing experience!"

 Words of Affirmation

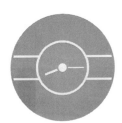 Quality Time

 Acts of Service

 Gifts

 Safe Touch

THE TRUE MEANING OF "LOVE"

Let's get started!

1. **What is your own definition of love?** (Write a sentence(s) or individual words to create your own definition.)

_____

_____

_____

_____

_____

In the definition that you wrote above, does it describe love as a verb, noun, or adjective? (Circle the one(s) that apply.)

VERB   NOUN   ADJECTIVE

2. **What makes you feel loved?** For this exercise *don't* spend a lot of time thinking about it! (Read the words and quickly place a check in two of the ovals. Draw a line from the two ovals you chose to the question mark.)

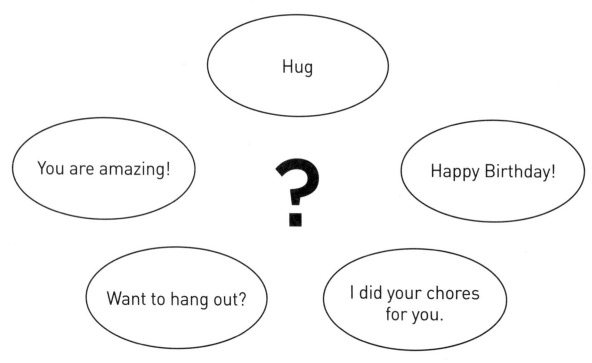

Name _____ Date _____

WORDS OF AFFIRMATION

○ *Makes me feel loved.*
○ *I like it.*

1. **Words of Affirmation** are truthful words that are spoken or written from one person to another that will uplift them and can make them feel good, encouraged, or loved. (Think of your own **Words of Affirmation** and place these words and symbols in the two boxes below. We have provided examples to get you started!)

◌◠ *Love Language* ◠◌

WORDS	**SYMBOLS OR PICTURE**
You are awesome!	♡

◠◌ *Opposite* ◌◠

2. **Harassment** hurts people's feelings and makes them feel bad. (In your own words, write three things that describe what you have learned about harassment.)

1. _____

2. _____

3. _____

NEGATIVE BEHAVIORS 🚫

Flattery is another example of negative behavior. People who use flattery are often NOT trusted by other people and are considered immature.

GRADES 5 & 6

Name _____ Date _____

QUALITY TIME

○ *Makes me feel loved.*
○ *I like it.*

What's in this for you? You are about to learn four techniques to become the best friend a person could ever want!

1. Quality time is _____ and _____ .

2. When you are trying to love someone with **Quality Time** you are intentionally and deliberately being around them to make them feel loved by giving them your time.
   In the four boxes on the left-hand side write the techniques that your teacher taught you.
   On the right-hand side explain "WHY" the technique is important:

FOUR QUALITY TIME TECHNIQUES: **EXPLAIN WHY THE TECHNIQUE IS IMPORTANT:**

FOUR QUALITY TIME TECHNIQUES	EXPLAIN WHY THE TECHNIQUE IS IMPORTANT
1.	1.
2.	2.
3.	3.
4.	4.

〜∽ *Discussion* ∽〜

3. Please answer the following question briefly: "If students at our school are regularly excluded or left out of activities, how can this negatively impact our school?" (Be prepared to have a discussion and support your ideas with examples.)

_____

_____

_____

_____

GRADES 5 & 6

Name _____ Date _____

ACTS OF SERVICE

○ *Makes me feel loved.*
○ *I like it.*

1. An **Act of Service** is doing something nice for someone that is_____,

_____, and _____.

2. ACTS OF SERVICE I CAN DO FOR MY:

FAMILY	SCHOOL

3. Take a moment and describe an Act of Service that someone did for you.

_____

_____

_____

_____

It takes two actions to help us be truly thankful:

1. We need to **be aware of what others are doing for us;**

2. We need to **do Acts of Service for others.**

ACTS OF SERVICE

1. The definition of **Acts of Service** is to do something kind for others by helping them out. The opposite would be doing something cruel to others or hurting them in some way. This could be verbally, emotionally, or physically. We call this negative behavior "bullying."

WHAT WOULD YOU DO TO STOP A BULLY?

A. I would tell them to _____ in a serious voice.

B. I would _____ or _____ away from the person.

C. If the person still follows me I would tell them to _____ in a serious voice.

D. If they continue to follow or bother me I would tell _____.

OUR SCHOOL TAKES SAFETY SERIOUSLY!

HERE IS A TEST TO SEE IF YOU KNOW SOME UNUSUAL FACTS ABOUT BULLYING.

TRUE or FALSE   If I see a bully hurting someone else, I should ignore it because it isn't really hurting me.

TRUE or FALSE   Sending a cruel text message could be a form of bullying.

TRUE or FALSE   If someone bullies a person in the neighborhood, it's not really the school's concern.

TRUE or FALSE   Bullies are always physically bigger than the person they are bullying.

ALWAYS REPORT BULLYING OR ANY DANGEROUS ACTIVITY to an adult. At school, this can be your teacher or anyone else who works at the school. At home, this can be any adult who is a family member, relative, or guardian.

STOP BULLIES! ALWAYS TELL SOMEONE!

ACTS OF SERVICE

1. The definition of **Acts of Service** is to do something kind for others by helping them out. The opposite would be to do something cruel to others or hurt them in some way. This could be verbally, emotionally, or physically. We call this negative behavior "bullying." (In the following shapes compare and contrast the difference between Acts of Service and Bullying. Write specific examples to show that you know the difference between each of them. One of the examples needs to involve cyber bullying.)

ACTS OF SERVICE	BULLYING BEHAVIOR
Example: Helping someone get up when they fall down.	*Example: Tripping someone.*

ALWAYS REPORT BULLYING OR ANY DANGEROUS ACTIVITY to an adult. At school, this can be your teacher or anyone else that works at the school. At home, this can be any adult that is a family member, relative, or guardian.

STOP BULLIES! ALWAYS TELL SOMEONE!

GITS

○ *Makes me feel loved.*
○ *I like it.*

1. Can you remember the best gift you ever received? Describe your gift and explain why you received it:

_____

_____

2. When you get a gift, can that gift itself love you? Think about the definition of loving someone and make an argument explaining why it's not the gift itself that makes a person feel loved:

_____

_____

_____

3. What are the three reasons that a gift makes someone feel loved?

A. _____

B. _____

C. _____

/ /

BRIBERY
HOME CONNECTION SECTION

Bribery is a negative behavior. It means that someone is trying to give a gift to get you to do something or get something from you. You should always ask your parents' permission before receiving a gift. If someone wants to give you a gift and you don't have permission then follow these three simple steps:

   A. Politely refuse the gift by saying, "No, thank you." Tell them that your parents don't allow you to take gifts or money without their permission.
   B. Tell your parents that someone offered you a gift.
   C. If someone in a car tries to offer you a gift to go with them, scream and run away. Try to find help. Do not spend any time talking to them and don't get close to their car.

SAFE TOUCH

○ *Makes me feel loved.*
○ *I like it.*

1. Thinking deeper: We know that babies require touch to be healthy, but why? Write your best prediction for why you believe touch is required for a baby to be healthy. Use scientific examples if you know of any.

_____

_____

_____

_____

2. Thinking about different cultures and different styles: What are some ways that you have observed people greeting each other or celebrating an accomplishment? For example, I've seen people give high fives after they make a goal playing soccer. Now it's your turn:

_____

_____

_____

_____

3. Obviously the way you use touch at home with your family or during sports is a lot different than when you are at school. List as many ways that you can think of that would be appropriate or considered safe touch at school. Your school rules should help you with the answers:

_____

_____

_____

_____

Everybody has a different comfort level when it comes to touch. Some people like to be touched and some people don't. Some people only like certain people to touch them. All people have a right to choose what their comfort level is. We need to be respectful of a person's personal space even if their love language is Touch.

Name _____ Date _____

TOUCH (PERSONAL SAFETY)

1. What are the three types of touch? (Hint: one of them is a "not safe" behavior)

   A. _____

   B. _____

   C. _____

2. If **unsafe** touch is going to happen to a child, it's usually done by someone they:

   A. _____

   B. _____

   C. _____

3. What are some reasons a child may not tell someone if a person they know, trust, or love touches them in an **unsafe** way?

   A. _____   B. _____

   C. _____   D. _____

   E. _____   F. _____

4. Who is the first person most kids tell when something bad happens to them?

   _____ but they should tell _____

5. If someone touches you or a friend in an **unsafe way**, you always need to tell at least two adults:

   A. An adult who lives in your _____.

   B. And an adult who works at _____.

Here are some good tips to be safe:
- Avoid situations where you might have to be alone with someone that you feel uneasy about. Tell your parents privately that you don't want to be with them.
- Follow your instincts. If it doesn't seem right then don't do it.
- If someone is bothering you, tell them to "Stop!" and draw your personal safety line.
- If you aren't sure about someone's behavior, ask your parents or an adult at school.

And remember, it's not likely to happen to you, so don't be afraid of everybody and everything. These lessons are to teach you how to be wise and safe!

GRADES 5 & 6

CHOOSING YOUR LOVE LANGUAGE
(ASSESSMENT)

For the following questions, statements, and actions circle the (x) if it makes you feel loved:

	WORDS OF AFFIRMATION	QUALITY TIME	ACTS OF SERVICE	GIFTS	SAFE TOUCH
HUGS					X
YOU ARE AMAZING	X				
I BOUGHT THIS FOR YOU				X	
I DID YOUR CHORES			X		
WANT TO HANG OUT AFTER SCHOOL?		X			
I MADE THIS FOR YOU				X	
YOU LOOK GREAT TODAY	X				
HIGH FIVE					X
I WILL CLEAN YOUR BEDROOM			X		
LET'S GO TO THE MOVIES		X			
GETTING YOUR BACK RUBBED					X
LET ME HELP YOU			X		
HAPPY BIRTHDAY				X	
THAT'S REALLY COOL	X				
WANT TO COME OVER TO MY HOUSE?		X			
GREAT JOB	X				
I KNEW YOU COLLECTED THESE, SO I BOUGHT ONE FOR YOU				X	
LET'S PLAY TOGETHER AT RECESS		X			
I LOADED THE DISHWASHER FOR YOU			X		
FIST BUMP					X
TOTAL OF X'S CIRCLED					

Name _____   Date _____

Love Language _____   Lesson# _____

NOTES AND REFLECTIONS JOURNAL

Summarizing/Notes: Taking notes isn't about writing every word that is taught by a teacher. In fact, that type of note-taking is not effective. Notes should be simple and meaningful to you. They are a way to help you remember the important points. Use meaningful words or symbols in the space below to help you remember today's lesson.

Reflecting: Reflecting is important because it means that you are actually thinking about what you learned. Please answer these questions: How will you use the information that you learned today? What personal goal will you set for yourself to practice using this information? How will you know that you have achieved your goal?

_____

_____

_____

_____

_____

_____

Want to Learn more?

Bridge 3 Resources, LLC is committed to providing educators with curriculum unlike any other in the world! Our research-based ideas and products educate the whole child—including complex, trauma sensitive, and highly capable learners—for academic excellence and life. We are committed to best practices in the classroom and creating connections between educators, students, peers, and families at the deepest levels.

Join our email list and get the latest information regarding future piloting opportunities, new releases, and current information.

www.BRIDGE3RESOURCES.com

About the Authors

Gary Chapman, Ph.D., is an author, speaker, and counselor who has a passion for people and helping them form lasting relationships. He is the #1 *New York Times* bestselling author of *The 5 Love Languages*® and the director of Marriage and Family Life Consultants, Inc. Gary travels the world presenting seminars and his radio programs air on more than 400 stations. For more information, visit 5lovelanguages.com.

D.M. Freed, M.Ed., believes a student's academic success hinges on the positive connections they build with their teacher, classmates, and family. As a former elementary teacher and in his current 18-year tenure as a school counselor with Central Valley School District (recipient of numerous "Outstanding Educational Excellence" awards) in the state of Washington, D.M.'s enthusiasm for helping young people succeed academically and in life has never waned. He holds an elementary education degree from Boise State University and two masters degrees in education from Whitworth University. For more information, visit bridge3resources.com.

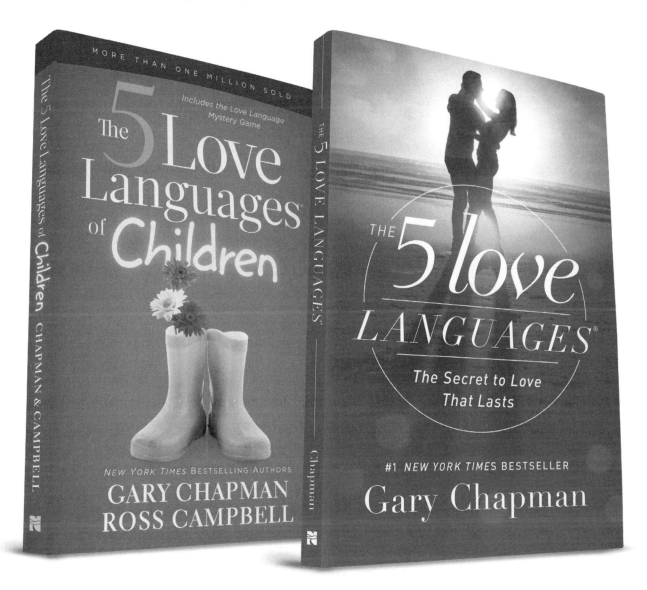

EMPOWERING ORGANIZATIONS BY

ENCOURAGING PEOPLE

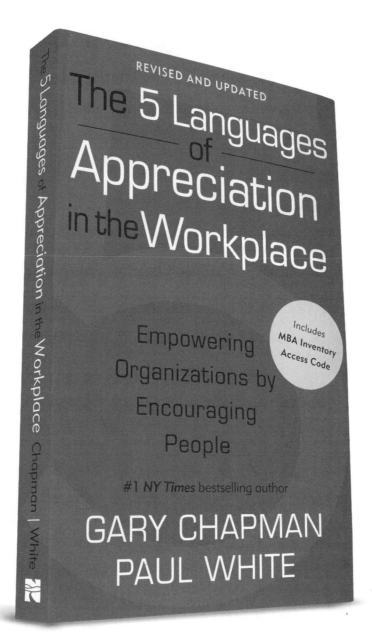

At work, people express and receive appreciation in different ways. If you try to express appreciation in ways that aren't meaningful to your co-workers, they may not feel valued at all. This is because you and your co-workers are speaking different languages. Based on the #1 *New York Times* bestseller, *The 5 Love Languages*®, Dr. Chapman and Dr. White give you practical steps to make any workplace environment more encouraging and productive. It's a helpful and practical resource for anyone working in an educational environment.

WWW.BRIDGE3RESOURCES.COM